W9-BRZ-000

FROM BROKEN GLASS

MY STORY OF FINDING HOPE IN HITLER'S DEATH CAMPS TO INSPIRE A NEW GENERATION

STEVE ROSS

With Glenn Frank and
Brian Wallace

hachette
BOOKS

NEW YORK   BOSTON

Copyright © 2018 by Steve Ross, Glenn Frank, and Brian Wallace

Jacket design by Carlos Esparza
Jacket photograph © Colin Walton/Alamy Images
Jacket copyright © 2018 by Hachette Book Group, Inc.

Hachette Book Group supports the right to free expression and the value of copyright. The purpose of copyright is to encourage writers and artists to produce the creative works that enrich our culture.

The scanning, uploading, and distribution of this book without permission is a theft of the author's intellectual property. If you would like permission to use material from the book (other than for review purposes), please contact permissions@hbgusa.com. Thank you for your support of the author's rights.

Hachette Books
Hachette Book Group
1290 Avenue of the Americas, New York, NY 10104
hachettebooks.com
twitter.com/hachettebooks

First edition: May 2018

Hachette Books is a division of Hachette Book Group, Inc. The Hachette Books name and logo are trademarks of Hachette Book Group, Inc.

The publisher is not responsible for websites (or their content) that are not owned by the publisher.

LCCN: 2017963705
ISBNs: 978-0-316-51304-3 (hardcover), 978-0-316-51308-1 (ebook)

Printed in the United States of America

LSC-C

10 9 8 7 6 5 4 3

To my mother, Basia

Contents

Foreword by Ray Flynn   ix

Introduction by Michael Ross   xiii

1. From Broken Glass   1

2. The Trouble in the World   3

3. A Life in America   9

4. Goodbye Lodz   15

5. Neighborhood Services   31

6. A Safe Way Out   37

7. A Friend in Boston   59

8. The Farm   65

9. Grandpa   75

10. The Forest   81

11. Memory and Escape   93

12. Dreaming of Home   99

13. The Man Who Lost His Way   113

Contents

14. Work and Death — 117

15. Intervention — 123

16. Self-Preservation — 127

17. Pinia — 143

18. Opening the Vault — 151

19. Herzil — 155

20. The End of Hope — 167

21. Heart Trouble — 173

22. Escape from Budzyn — 177

23. Radom — 179

24. No Matter How Bad — 189

25. The Honor of Work — 193

26. The Train to Auschwitz — 199

27. How I Learned of Robert Hall — 203

28. Tattooed — 211

29. Matriculation — 219

30. An Empire Falls — 223

31. Dead, Gone, and Forgotten — 227

32. The Busing Crisis — 231

33. Guns in the Distance — 237

34. To Never Forget — 241

35. Memorial Rising — 249

36. Liberation — 253

Acknowledgments — 263

Foreword

Szmulek Rozental was a boy, an orphan, and a refugee when he arrived in Boston in 1949. At the time, he suffered from tuberculosis, the mildest of the wounds he bore from his years in ten Nazi death camps. He had come through horrors that no person, and certainly no child, should ever have to endure.

In Boston, he would remake himself from a sickly survivor to an all-American hero.

Steve's story came to stand as a testament to the freedom and liberty that too many of us take for granted. He understood what America stood for long before he set foot on the nation's soil, cherishing the small American flag given him by a US soldier in Europe. He relished the opportunity to raise children here free from fear and want. He earned an advanced degree in psychology so he could help others who suffered. He would spend the balance of his life giving back. But he wanted something more, something utterly essential for the survival of his own spirit and for the memory of his and so many others' families: for Americans, and Bostonians especially, to learn and remember the lessons of that special scourge known as the Shoah. He demanded that we never forget the hatred, nor the power of hope. He understood that the right memorial could express those fundamental principles.

That's where I came into Steve's story.

I knew Steve from when both of us were youth outreach workers in the streets of South Boston and Dorchester. Steve was a beloved figure among the kids he mentored. When I ran for mayor the first time, in 1983, several of "Steve's kids" were with me. They shared my philosophy that government should serve everybody, most of all those who work hard to raise families and must scrape from one paycheck to the next. They believed in building bridges, the way Steve and I were trying to do, between diverse neighborhoods and long-suffering communities.

By the time he came to see me about his vision for a Holocaust memorial, Steve already was a hero of our mayoral administration. People kept shaking his hand and hugging him as he sat in the lobby. In his mind, however, he was just Szmulek Rozental from Lodz, Poland, a shtetl kid coming hat in hand to the mayor's office.

We talked about the past and the future that morning as we looked out over historic Dock Square. What the memorial would look like was still to be determined. But where it should be seemed instantly clear to both of us. When I said I agreed that it should go on the mall between Union and Congress Streets, where it would make a statement as dramatic as the history it would honor, Steve's eyes lit up. He envisioned the memorial standing shoulder-to-shoulder with Boston's emblems of liberty and social justice.

From the mayor's office, we could see Faneuil Hall, with its second-floor room that will be known forever as the Cradle of Liberty. Peter Faneuil, a refugee like Steve, had given the city a building where abolitionists would light the fuse that became the war to end slavery. A century later, another child of Boston, John F. Kennedy, delivered an election-eve speech there in which he vowed to be "the champion of the aged, and of children, and the handicapped, and the friend of those who have been forgotten, of those who have not been remembered, of those who have needed a helping hand, and of those who needed a good neighbor."

In front of the hall stands the statue of Samuel Adams, looking ready to once again take up the fight for freedom and liberty. Adams wrote and spoke thousands of words championing liberty and freedoms, but none were more powerful than his simple rejoinder when someone tried to make a "gift" to his family of a woman kept in human bondage. "A slave cannot live in my house. If she comes she must be free."

Mere feet from Mr. Adams sits James Michael Curley, dressed in his typical three-piece suit. In life, he often crowned his outfit with a perfectly blocked homburg. But he grew up not in finery but in dire poverty. His parents escaped death and starvation in Ireland by making their way to Boston. Both parents were refugees, having survived the "coffin ships" to start a new life in Boston, just as Steve Ross would. Jim Curley gave back as our "Mayor of the Poor." He built public schools and health centers, public beaches and public baths.

Just out of view of the memorial is the place where a black man and an Irishman became the first to die in our War of Independence. Both were gunned down by English troops in front of the Old State House in the Boston Massacre.

The Holocaust memorial, I said that morning, had to be in that historic company. And so it is, thanks most of all to Steve Ross. The rest, as you can see by the six towers that bear witness there today and by this magnificent book that brims with Steve's moral voice, is history.

> —*Ray Flynn is the former mayor of Boston and*
> *US ambassador to the Vatican*

Introduction

The road from Warsaw to Krasnik was heavy with gloom. Along it, miles of forests, filled with arrow-straight deciduous trees, merged into the gray winter sky. Occasionally, a small farmhouse would dot the landscape.

On that day, it was cold with a wet snow falling. It was seventy-one years after the Holocaust. It happened to be my birthday, but it felt joyless as my mind was elsewhere. I was imagining how cold my father, Steve Ross, must have been, surviving five of these winters, wearing only paper-thin pajamas. These were the woods he attempted to hide in, only to be captured by Nazis and sent to a series of ten concentration camps until his liberation from Dachau on April 29, 1945.

The purpose of my visit to Krasnik was to trace the final days of my father's murdered family—my grandparents, six aunts and uncles, and two cousins. After the Nazis arrived in Lodz in September 1939, my father, then an eight-year-old boy, and his family fled from their home with whatever possessions they could carry. They headed eastward, attempting to reach the Russian border. Instead, they were trapped in Krasnik, a small town near Lublin.

My guidepost in tracing my father's steps was his recent manuscript, which had been painstakingly assembled by a team of dedicated friends and writers. The story of his life, now the subject of this book, is what directed my steps to learn my family's past, and in so doing to better understand my own.

Arriving at the small archives office, I was struck by how the bureaucratic workers emotionlessly processed our slips of papers. They returned with giant stacks of dusty ledgers, the ruled pages inside filled with barely legible handwritten notations, fading from decades of age.

For hours, three of us—me, my fiancée Karolina, and our guide Krysztof—pored over the books, nibbling on the leftover breakfast rolls we'd tucked into our bags. Turning the brittle pages, I suddenly came across a page with rows of the name Rozental, my father's surname before it was changed to Ross by US immigration officials. Tracing the rows of my family's names across the page, under the column listing the next place of residence were the letters *ND*—the Polish abbreviation for *nie dotyczy*, meaning "does not apply." I understood, then, that this was all that was left of my family.

A wave of emotion hit me, and uncontrollably I wept, while Karolina tried to console me with her embrace. It wasn't that I had believed my relatives had somehow survived; rather, I was struck by the complicit documentation of murder, and realized that this cold page would serve as the closest thing to a final resting place where I could mourn.

I learned something else that day—something hopeful amid a period of hopelessness. In the final days before the liquidation of the Krasnik ghetto, when the remaining Jews were sent to concentration camps, my grandmother sensed the end was near. She made the extraordinary decision to give away her youngest child—my father—in the hope that he might survive.

Knocking on the door of a family she'd never met, she pleaded with them to take young Szmulek. Reluctantly they did, despite reports of neighbors being sentenced to death for harboring Jews.

With this decision, the family of farmers saved my father's life. In the few months that he was with them, he avoided the same fate of my grandparents, aunts and uncles, and cousins. While he would go on to endure unthinkable cruelty, starvation, and torture, he would survive, as would his eldest brother, whom I would know as my uncle Harry.

And so my search began anew. This time I was searching not for my family, but for the strangers who'd saved my father's life. I learned their name was Sadowsky. As this book was being published, our guide Krysztof was actively searching archived public school records to find the family's descendants. I would want them to know that the act of taking my father into the family home that day is why he survived, and why our family—myself, my sister Julie, and her son Joseph—are alive today.

My father had been searching for another man as well. Throughout his life, one person had served as his greatest influence. Although he'd met the man only briefly, that brief moment rekindled his will to live.

It was an American tank commander who liberated Dachau. When he saw young Szmulek Rozental walking past him, he hopped off his tank, put his arms around my father, and spoke the first kind words he had heard in five bitter years. He held him and gave him food to eat.

My father spoke about it on the television series *Unsolved Mysteries* as he was searching for the soldier.

"He looked to me as though he was rough and tough, and yet he knew how to put his arm around me, at that time in my life, when nobody's ever done that before," he said.

"If I could ever find that soldier, I would say to him that he is part of my life. He would be part of my family. I would want him to know that what he has done for me... I emulated, and that I love people because of him."

My father would spend his entire life searching for

him. While doing so, he was never without the forty-eight-star American flag that the soldier gave to him. That flag, some additional details that he recalled, and a tireless passion to be reunited with his liberator are all part of my father's story as told here.

The story, of course, includes his improbable survival through Hitler's death camps, including his escape from Auschwitz. It also includes what he did when he arrived in the United States, and how he spent every waking minute giving back to the country that had freed him from the gates of Hell.

He gave back by working as a social worker on the streets of Boston: attending to at-risk youth, making sure they went to school and later to college. He helped thousands of kids with a driven intensity. By fixing the broken lives of others, he, in a way, could fix his own.

Later in life, many of those he helped and worked with had become successful business leaders, attorneys, and legislators. Together, along with the help of Boston's Mayor Ray Flynn, they allowed him to fulfill his dream of building a memorial to those who perished. A place for him—and all of us—to mourn the family we lost. Today the New England Holocaust Memorial sits prominently along Boston's Freedom Trail, and is visited by millions of people each year.

In 2017, the memorial took on a most unfortunate designation—a victim of anti-Semitism. For twenty-two years the nearly all-glass edifice stood as a gleaming memorial to both the memory of a people and the values held by the community in which it sits. But just days after white nationalists marched in Charlottesville, Virginia, chanting "Jews will not replace us" and left injury and death in their wake, one of the memorial's panels was shattered in an act of vandalism in the dark of night. It was the second time that summer a panel was destroyed. This vandalism—along with the news that far-right activists were planning a Boston-based follow-up rally to the one that had turned deadly in Charlottesville—inspired a counterprotest by 50,000 people who marched into downtown Boston the following weekend to stand up against hatred. At the rededication of the memorial, my father and I listened as the speakers made references to Kristallnacht—the Night of Broken Glass—the bloody Berlin pogrom that revealed to the world the true intent of Hitler's plans for the Jewish people. It was not lost on any of those in attendance that, here again, we were forced to rebuild from broken glass. But we would not allow ourselves to rediscover how easily a society can slide into violence. As the German Jewish poet Heinrich Heine wrote in 1820, "Where they burn books, they will also ultimately burn people." We didn't need anyone to remind us that the same might be said of places where anyone tolerates the shattering of our treasures.

That the memorial was desecrated twice during the writing of this book only makes me firmer in my belief that everyone throughout the world should know this story, not only so that we can learn more about the darkest chapter in human history, but also so that we can work together to create a world where such an atrocity as the Holocaust can never be repeated. I hope, too, that readers will learn how every single act of kindness, bravery, and defiance, no matter how small, can inspire hope and renewal for generations to come.

—*Michael Ross*

FROM
BROKEN GLASS

Chapter 1

From Broken Glass

People say the phrase all the time: *Never forget. Never forget.* They say it in synagogues on the Sabbath and in churches when they talk about cruelty in the world. They say it whenever a Holocaust survivor passes on, at memorial events across the country. *Never forget. Never forget.* Famous people have created foundations so that we all never forget. Even some of the concentration camps are now preserved as museums so that people remember what happened there.

Sometimes when *I* think of those words I get confused. I know they mean that we don't want our sons and daughters and grandchildren to fail to remember the truth, and that we want those who hold power to understand that this cannot be allowed to happen again. I know the phrase means that we want future generations of people all over the world to withstand the powers of hate; to stand up to indignities; to not let any one group of people be blamed for the wrongs of the world and be subject to extermination. I know all that. And I want those things, too.

But sometimes, I think to myself, I would do anything to forget.

I want so badly to forget that it makes me cry. I wish for just one day, for one hour, or even a single moment, I could be free of the memories; I wish I could feel like what happened to me never occurred; I wish I could erase it all and have a few hours of precious peace. The refrain *Never forget* sometimes sounds to me like my curse. I know in my heart this is selfish. I know others have endured as much as or more than I have; I knew so many who never made it. I am eighty-seven years old now, and I remain searching for that moment when I am able to forget the people we lost.

My name is Steve Ross, though that is not the name I first knew. When I was born I was Szmulek Rozental. My life began in Lodz, Poland, in 1931.

Chapter 2

The Trouble in the World

Lodz, Poland
Summer 1939

When you're eight, you do not understand that the world has trouble in it. You do not realize how your life can change in just an instant. You do not see that bad things can happen. I was eight in 1939.

That summer did not seem different to me from any summer that had come before it. July and August were dry and warm; Kammiena #3, our street, seemed dusty and sticky; and the sun stayed out late and rose early over our apartment. Wagons and horses made their familiar and constant clatter on the parched cobblestones, the animals and their loads carrying food and wares from one enclave to another. Polish soldiers often rode or walked by our yard as well, some looking stern and mean, but others, in groups, laughing or pushing at their friends. My grandmother and my mother always stopped whatever they were doing in the kitchen when they heard the soldiers talking outside. Nervous creases crossed their faces, and I wondered why they looked so scared. "Don't worry, Babsa," I shouted to my grandmother as I raced outside to see where the soldiers were going. I hoped somehow that I could make friends with them and keep my family from having to be concerned.

"Szmulek, come back at once," my mother would shout. "Those are not nice men."

Our apartment was on the third floor of a three-story walk-up, and the wooden stairs creaked and groaned with every step. My legs were small and my shoes were often worn and tattered, but to keep Mrs. Tzilcic from yelling when I passed I tried to jump from landing to landing, hoping she and the other the mothers and grandmothers in our building wouldn't stop what they were doing and scold me for making noise. "We can't sleep at night with your family upstairs," Mrs. Tzilcic called out to me. "There are too many people crowded into your tiny space, all snoring and shifting around above us. Even Grandma Jietta is complaining from this." I was fairly certain Grandma Jietta did not complain. Not a day ever went by in winter or summer when she was not perched in the window watching my friends and me playing in the yard, a smile on her face we could all see clearly even three floors below. We always waved, and she always waved back.

"Mrs. Tzilcic said we make too much noise at night," I told my brother Herzil. "She said we keep Grandma Jietta awake at night."

"Mrs. Tzilcic is a nag," he said. "Grandma Jietta is deaf and her legs don't work. Besides, she likes us."

The yard at the front of our building was flat and wide, and Kammiena #3 was covered in concrete. My father would spend all day running the village butcher shop around the corner, and when we were done with shul I would hang out in the backyard with our neighbor Pinia, whose father was the local baker.

I could not remember a day when Pinia and I were not together. He had a round face and red cheeks, hair like a floppy brown hat rising from his head and sagging forward near his eyes. He was always smiling and looking expectant, as if something wonderful lay over the horizon, and whenever anyone dared to tease or scold us, he would puff up his chest in defiance.

"This is Szmulek, and when he grows up he will be better than you," he'd say. "He will be a great man." Sometimes he would call me "the philosopher king." I have no idea where he got these ideas, but it always made me laugh when he expressed them—out of bashful embarrassment if nothing else. Then Pinia would grin at me and nod as if to say: Let's go. I've told them what is going to happen.

We didn't have toys, so we spent hours flipping nuts or teaching each other songs, and when the unusual happened and an automobile or a truck rumbled by, we chased after it hoping desperately to inhale the smell of the strange new gas engines and feel the smoke on our tongues. When we did we jumped and giggled and squinted at our good fortune, then dodged the horses and farm carts that were agitated by the loud and fast machines that had passed them.

At some point in the evening my father would return, the tang of blood wafting into the house behind him. He would find me in the yard and kiss me, and I would feel the whiskers of his beard tickle my cheeks. Gray had begun to streak onto his beard and sideburns, and his eyes were deep and kind and tired. "I will kiss you until your nose wears down to just a nub," he would say.

Though his meat cutting did not make him large profits, in the Talmud he found enough to fill his heart. "Study," he told me, "and the words of God will tell you what to do." He studied long and hard and I think now and then that he prayed he would always be able to feed his family. "God always has a reason," he would sometimes say. And though there was much truth to what he taught me, I've found that last lesson the hardest to unlearn.

I was the youngest child. My parents were in their forties by the time they'd had me. I don't think I was planned, but it didn't matter.

My older brother, Herzil, was in charge of the electricity at the synagogue.

I remember being filled with joy and laughter when I saw him finish wiring the building and turn on the first bulb he'd installed. It was the night before the Sabbath service and the sanctuary was empty. "Magic," he told me when the bulb began to glow, and I believed him.

Two of my sisters, Bella and Lonia, lived in other apartments, though not too far away, and they each had three children and lives of their own but my mother and Babsa in particular worried for them often. "Abe says the Germans will come and that they are dangerous," Babsa said, repeating what one of her friends had warned over and over, every time he came to the house.

"Not in front of Szmulek," my mother said. "Later we will discuss the Germans."

Chapter 3

A Life in America

Boston, Massachusetts
September 1995

In the many decades I've spent in Boston, I've taken part in projects I never dreamed I'd live to work on, shaken the hands of political leaders that I'd been taught by the Nazi guards and capos throughout my childhood would never want to associate with a person like me, and had the blessing of working with students in some of the city's toughest neighborhoods and finding myself as inspired by them as I hope they were by me. But spearheading the creation of the New England Holocaust Memorial—what would become one of Boston's most visited landmarks—is the thing that I am most proud of.

To be sure, I am not alone responsible. The effort to build a memorial in Boston was carried forth by the many people who donated money and time and energy, the politicians who helped smooth the path, the corporations that gave assistance, and the volunteers who worked so hard to push the initiative ahead. Still, notwithstanding their undoubtedly crucial efforts, I *do* feel responsible for the memorial in a certain way. And not just because I talked to mayors and local executives and celebrities and convinced them to work together to support it; not just because I worked for years to get the right design and to find the right location and to convince everyone that the money would be there. No, I feel responsible for it because for decades before this day I have felt answerable to the fact that it didn't exist, the fact that another year had passed without my family and friends, and the millions of victims I never got the chance to meet, being properly remembered. I am responsible for ensuring the memorial forever stands tall in the heart of the city because I survived.

I am the one who passed through ten concentration camps, starved nearly to death, overcame beatings and sexual abuse, poisoning and terror. I am the one who lived, somehow. Not my brothers and sisters, not my mother and father, not my nieces and nephews, my grandmother, my neighbors, or my friends. Some mornings I still jolt when I wake and remember what happened—that all of them are gone.

What makes the fact of my survival more painful are the reasons that I endured: none, so far as I can gather. I am simply lucky. I am not possessed of any extraordinary skills of pain endurance. I am not stronger than anyone else. I cry and feel agony just like everyone in the world.

People have challenged me throughout my life about my sense of luck. "You are the most unlucky person I know," I've been told. True, I was orphaned by the Holocaust, broken and made witness to—and in a few cases that I wish I could forget, made the target of—cruelties beyond the imagination. But the people who don't recognize my luck can't see what I see: that I am here and six million others who endured everything I did had to also give up the biggest thing of all—their lives.

That sense of hopefulness in the face of hardship—combined with the lessons I learned from fellow death camp prisoners about moral courage and human tenderness—is something I tried always to bring to my forty-year career as a public youth counselor working in some of Boston's poorest neighborhoods.

To all the students who listened, I would tell my story and show that if I can survive what I did, they can face their own struggles, come to grips with the injustices they're up against, and fight to overcome them, maybe even to prosper.

"Why do you think you lived when everyone else died?" I've been asked several times.

"What was it like to work in the incinerator, shoveling the ashes of people you knew?"

"How did you have the courage to hide in the latrine, burying yourself in human shit and piss?"

"Do you ever feel guilt about cutting the line to try to get enough water to survive?"

I would answer every painful question.

Every time I shared my story, I would feel the air shift as I started describing life in the camps, as if I were being transported back there and the students I spoke with were following me through the camp gates. It didn't matter if the schools I visited were crumbling or overcrowded, the students gathered around me on a gymnasium floor. Their eyes opened wider, conversations stopped. Feet ceased tapping. Eyebrows furrowed.

I still sometimes return to the schools I once worked at to speak to the students, and now I will add a new ending to my story. I will tell them how politicians worked together with the Jewish community to get momentum for our memorial, about how we launched a design competition and selected the six glass towers you see today, about how we manufactured extra glass panes, and about how one special day, the day before the memorial's dedication, I asked my wife, Mary, my love of thirty-two years, if we could sleep there, out under the stars. Just to feel part of it. She came with me and brought sleeping bags and blankets. The stone of the memorial was cold and hard under our backs. Our children joined us, and some of their friends, too. "We are going to stay with you," they said, and no matter how much we argued, they wouldn't leave us and go to their warm beds.

I never told my children of the memory from sixty years prior that came back to me that night in downtown Boston. I was eight and it was autumn in Lodz, and my mother agreed we could have an adventure. Pulling on warm clothes and grabbing my older brother's long coats, we crept outside searching for a sukkah, a holiday trellis erected to celebrate new beginnings. No one had built one, but we were not interested in anything but sleeping outside. A farmer's wagon filled with hay became our campground and we slept there buried under the dried stalks.

Cool breezes seemed to sweep over us from every direction, sweet smells drifting from people's woodstoves. This was home, what my childhood was going to be.

Lying under the stars, staring up at the towers of the memorial, I tried to hold the memory of the farmer's wagon in my head. I wanted to stay there, in that sweet moment of my past, as long as I could. I wanted to remember my brother's face and his laugh. I wanted to remember my mother wrapping bread with sugar for us to eat outside. I tried to remember my father warning us to be careful. I tried to focus on my dear family.

Memory, though, sometimes has its own way. What I remembered was the bustling in the distance of soldiers' boots.

Chapter 4

Goodbye Lodz

Lodz, Poland
September 8, 1939

The ground in the yard trembled in a way I had not felt before. The occasional truck that had gone by in the past had clattered and sputtered, but this was altogether different. Herzil stopped running with me and his head turned at an angle, as if he could better make out the sound if one ear was tilted closer to the concrete. An anxious look descended over his face.

"Herzil?" I said. "Keep playing."

His expression confused me. We didn't get to run and chase in the yard too often since he was home only rarely. "Herzil, chase me again."

"Hush, Szmulek," he replied.

I was uneasy.

"Herzil?" I said again.

"Little brother, be quiet," he scolded me.

Several neighbors appeared in their windows, looking back and forth down Kammiena #3. Two horses tied in the yard began to bray and pull against their bindings, their back ends lurching about as their rear hooves tapped the ground beneath them. Pinia's father came out of the bakery, brushing flour off his apron, and looked bewildered.

"Are Mama and Papa home?" Herzil asked.

"Yes," I said.

I hoped the rumbling would stop. My body seemed like it was vibrating in rhythm with the ground; my heart beat in my ears and throat.

"Szmulek, come here," Herzil said. "Move away from the street." He began to back up toward the buildings and I realized he was pulling me back with him, his fist around my collar, my legs nearly sliding over the cement yard.

A truck thundered by, its back open to the air where twenty soldiers in yellow uniforms sat in rows, rifles between their knees. A man on his way to evening services at the shul came out of the apartment building and halted abruptly. He squinted at the vehicle, following it as it traveled across the area in front of the yard and disappeared down Kammiena #3. He peered at Herzil and me, still squinting suspiciously, as if we'd somehow made the truck appear.

"And how many have passed?" he asked.

"That is the first," Herzil said.

Stretching his neck, the man stared straight ahead. I could barely hear him now over the patter of the engines. "There will be more," he said. He turned and went back inside.

Three more trucks shuddered over the cobblestones, rushing toward some destination I could not imagine. I heard Herzil mumbling: "Keep going. Keep going. Keep going," as each truck passed. I looked up at him and my heart beat even faster.

"The rabbi told Papa we didn't have to worry. Don't you remember?" I said, staring at his concerned face. "Herzil, they will have paper uniforms on and be nice to us."

"I don't think those soldiers are wearing paper," he said.

I turned back to the street. My stomach tightened. The last truck had stopped. The brakes released a belch of smoke or steam and for a moment there was no movement. Paper uniforms, I thought to myself. They do not want to hurt us. Finally, the door to the cabin swung open and a soldier in a pressed brown shirt stepped out onto the platform below the truck door. He leaned in to speak to the driver; and after this there was a grinding sound of metal on metal until the truck began to back up. The soldier's hand went up and the truck stopped. With a lurch, it then turned into the yard.

"Go upstairs, Szmulek," Herzil said.

"I don't want to," I replied.

Jumping from the platform, the soldier in the brown uniform shrugged and wiped at his lapels. He nodded to one of the men in the back, who immediately shouted in German. One by one the soldiers jumped to the ground, forming a line facing the apartments. Their rifles were pressed against their chests.

Quiet descended over the yard. I could hear my own breathing and realized that the engine rumbling had stopped. I imagined trucks and soldiers at every other yard on Kammiena #3 and wondered if any other boys were watching them like I was.

A Polish policeman on horseback appeared from behind one of the apartment buildings, followed by five other policemen on foot. Their uniforms were gray and dirty and I wondered whether they felt bad to be so messy when the soldiers looked clean and orderly. These policemen pulled a wobbly wooden farmer's cart behind them, struggling under the weight. The cart was filled with blankets. After setting it down in the center of the yard, they backed up and stood behind the soldiers. I wondered why they looked so frightened. Some of them I recognized; I'd seen them before, on the streets while walking to Papa's shop or seder. I waved. None of them waved back. One of them turned away and stared at the ground.

At the far end of the yard, four Hassidic men I'd seen a few weeks earlier had gathered near the entrance to their building. They began to pray, davening and reciting passages in hushed tones. Another man stepped out from behind the men praying. "And why are you here in this yard?" he shouted. "We have done nothing wrong." He paused when there was no response. "These people have done nothing wrong," he said, pointing to the Hassidic men. "There are many children here, also," he pleaded, his voice fading off.

"Why did he say that?" I asked Herzil. "Why did he tell them there are children here?" I could feel Herzil's fingers still gripping the back of my collar, and I tried to wiggle free so I could get an answer to my question. He did not let go.

Staring at the buildings while he paced, the soldier in the brown uniform pressed his hands together and raised them to his lips as if he were praying. The soles of his black, nearly knee-high boots rapped against the ground with each step. An armband in red and black had a symbol on it I did not recognize. On his hat was a badge that looked like an eagle or a falcon, the wings outstretched. He had light hair and a pointed chin. His nose was thin and straight. His appearance worried me for reasons I could not make clear in my head.

A few other residents had gathered in the yard. Pinia came out of the bakery and ran over to Herzil and me. Another woman left the shop and huddled in the doorway clutching three small children. I peered up at Herzil, whose expression had not changed.

"The rabbi said they aren't going to hurt us. I heard him say it," I said to Pinia.

"So why, then, do they need these rifles?" I heard someone say nearby. "Are we so threatening?"

Signaling for quiet, the soldier's hand went up. When he reached the policeman on horseback, he nodded to him and patted the horse's neck and mane. Another soldier appeared from the cabin of the truck and ran to them with a cone for making speeches to a crowd.

"These soldiers will not be here long," the policeman announced through the cone. "Cooperate with them and we can all go home in peace."

I could see people gazing out their windows now.

"Are the rifles necessary?" someone asked.

"We want to keep order," the policeman said. "That is all." Moving quickly, the other policemen pulled blankets from the cart and spread them in a square, centered in the yard.

"What do you want from us?" The voice came from a window above me. "Why are you here tonight?"

I wondered about Lonia and Bella and my nieces and nephews. Were there soldiers in their yard? They didn't have Herzil with them. What if they were afraid? I thought about running the four blocks to their house, but Herzil's grip was too tight.

"You are no longer allowed to have any valuables," the policeman announced. "Jewelry, anything made of gold or silver, silk, stockings, anything of value. Gather these things and bring them out. Everyone must do this at once. Go into your homes and bring the valuables down and place them on the blankets. If you do this the soldiers will leave you alone."

"Just like that," one of the neighbors said. "You make this announcement and then steal our property? Who are these men? Why are you helping them rob us?"

"Go back to your homes now," the policeman shouted. "Go. Gather these items and bring them here."

"Go lock your doors," another man yelled to those in the yard and those listening from their windows. "These golems cannot take from us."

A sickening feeling rose in my throat. I didn't like the yelling. I didn't want Papa and Mama to bring out their menorah or their candlesticks or the silk socks I had recently purchased. But I was afraid now. I was trembling. "Herzil?" I said.

"Shh," he said in a whisper.

The yard was filled with voices; so many I could not understand what was being said by anyone. The four Hassidic men were waving their arms at the policemen and scolding them and pointing fingers. Pinia's father, the baker, seemed to be screaming at him to go back to the shop. Others seemed to be running but in no particular direction.

"Why do they want our things?" I asked Herzil. "They

are ours. Why do they think they aren't ours anymore?" I tried to remember the rabbi's words, hoping that if I could recall them they would come true. Papa believed him, so I did, too. The rabbi spoke God's words. He knew God. He talked to him all the time.

My sisters each had a pretty comb for their hair. Did these soldiers want those things, too? "Please don't let them take Anka's combs," I said to Herzil.

The policeman was screaming for quiet, bellowing through the cone in all directions. The soldier in the brown uniform watched warily, his eyes narrowing. I could see he was growing impatient. With a nod, he signaled to the other policemen pointing to the Hassidic men, then shut his eyes as if he was very tired.

I imagined my nieces and nephews rushing through their apartment gathering their things and huddling under their table with their mother and father. Something told me they were not safe. "Lonia and Bella?" I said to Herzil.

"Szmulek, do not speak," Herzil ordered.

Descending upon the Hassidic men, the policemen pushed and pulled them toward the edge of the yard. One man's shtreimel fell off; another man's tallit fell to the ground and was kicked to the side. The Hassids tripped and stumbled but finally complied and stood in a row, facing us. They looked at one another and at the other residents. Everyone was confused by what was happening.

One by one a policeman tied their hands behind their backs. They each complained that they were being hurt; that the ropes were too tight; that tying was unnecessary.

Residents protested but the complaints ebbed until there were only whispers. I looked at Herzil and at Pinia, both of whom looked terrified. A woman, the wife of one of the Hassidic men, ran from the doorway and fell at her husband's feet, turning to the policeman on horseback and the soldier in the brown uniform, begging them to let her husband go. The soldier picked her up by the arm, turned her toward the apartments, and kicked her in the back, sending her sprawling across the yard. He screamed out in German but we did not understand.

Circling the truck, the policeman on horseback reappeared from behind the cab with lighters, each glowing with flame. Leaning down, he spoke to the German, who signaled to several of his men to take the devices. They did and each of the soldiers stared at the fire in his possession, looking flush and appreciative of this officer's trust.

Lecturing the crowd, again—though still using a language unfamiliar to me—the soldier in the brown uniform seemed as if he was trying to be calm and reasoned. To me, though, he looked wicked, methodical, purposeful; as if he believed in what he was doing—believed in stealing from others and threatening people—acting as if he was doing what needed to be done.

I felt Pinia take my hand. I squeezed back.

The soldier paused, let the silence take over; wanting the quiet, I think, to fill everyone's ears for a moment before the chaos that was coming.

Screaming was all I heard next, from all around me, from everywhere. With a wave of the lighters the soldiers had ignited the beards and the collars of the Hassidic men, engulfing their faces in flames. They writhed in pain and shrieked, two of them falling to the ground trying to rub the fire from their faces on the concrete. The smell of their burning flesh pierced my nose. Pinia vomited.

Several residents pressed forward to try to help the men but the soldier glared at them and they moved back. The other two Hassidic men dropped to their knees, their faces sizzling, yellow embers floating up from their scalps and disappearing. They gasped for air, breathing in flames, smoke rising from their shoulders.

One of the soldiers laughed, still standing with his gun pressed to his chest. Another glared as if to say the burned men deserved to be tortured.

I began to cry, and moved even closer to Herzil as Pinia started to weep as well. I put my arm around my friend and held him. Why was this happening? I was terrified I would be next or that Herzil would be ignited, or Papa. Babsa was older like the Hassidic men were. Did they only burn older people? Did they only burn people with long beards? Papa's beard was not nearly as long as those of the Hassidic men. My body shook with terror.

The policeman was screaming again through the cone, demanding valuables, urging everyone to hurry. The soldiers with the guns would go house to house, he said, and gather the items if they were not brought down immediately and placed on the blankets. "Go now. Go," he ordered. "Quickly."

Residents began to emerge from the doorways of the apartments, hugging silk blouses or candlesticks or clocks to their chests. They formed a line and slowly paced by the growing pile, gently placing their possessions on top, gazing at their valuables as they walked away. Most were crying. Some were shaking. Everyone was uncertain, shocked, and sad. My parents came out, ran to the front of the line, dropped a mirror and several silver platters onto the mass of valuables, then ran to us and tried to wipe away my tears.

"This is the end of the world," my mother said.

The pile angled forward as the items stacked up and toppled toward one side. Cantering back and forth inspecting the haul, the policeman seemed pleased. After kicking several items to level out the load, he was berated by the soldier in the brown uniform apparently for possibly causing damage. They glared at one another.

Many of the neighbors had gathered near the burned men and were trying to remove their singed clothing. Blisters and peeling skin was all I could see. I wondered whether they were dead. My mother tried to press my eyes into her blouse so I would not have to see the grisly results of the Germans' work. "Szmulek, do not look." She was crying. Herzil was holding my father by the belt.

Shouts of protest erupted and I pushed away. The soldier in the brown uniform and several of his men were pointing at the upper floors of our building, bellowing orders and instructions, repeating their words over and over, their tone growing harsher as they kept yelling. People scattered around us began arguing with them, hollering and pleading, so many talking at once I could not understand what was being said. Even my father started to call out to them but he was drowned out by the noise.

At a gallop, six soldiers burst from the line and disappeared into the building.

"She's old and deaf," I finally heard someone say. "Crippled."

I could hear their boots on the stairs. I could see the other soldiers pointing and gesturing. I watched the policeman on horseback settle back into his saddle and peer upward, expressionless. Even those tending to the burned men turned their attention to this commotion.

I looked up in time to see a window on the upper floor shattering and a person in a chair flying through it, spewing glass, twisting in the air. The crowd below spread as if a drop of water had fallen in a still pond. The body crumpled against the yard under the chair. Blood shot across the concrete. It was Grandma Jietta. She hadn't brought down her valuables.

Please don't hurt my parents. Please don't hurt my family, I thought. Please. Please.

"Mama? Papa?" I didn't know what I wanted to ask them. I think I just wanted to hear their voices. To make sure they were still there, even though they were next to me.

With a gasp, my mother covered her mouth. She was staring out into the yard where the soldiers had burst outside of our building after murdering Grandma Jietta. They were not finished. Lifting him off his feet, they carried our neighbor Grocia, who struggled to free himself. His wife and two small children trailed behind them screaming to let him go. The children were sobbing even harder than I was. Grocia's long black coat tore at the sleeves and his wide-brimmed hat flew off behind him. His legs tried to run even though he was off the ground. He was dropped at the foot of the soldier in the brown uniform, who signaled to his men to pick him up again.

"God help us," my mother said.

His horse bucking behind him, the policemen approached Grocia. Grocia leaned back in fear of being trampled. "You were stealing," the policemen said. "You're a thief."

"I stole nothing," Grocia said.

"Tell us where you have hidden the valuables you have stolen," the policeman said.

Grocia's daughter pulled away from her mother, wrapping her arms around her father's leg before being pulled away by a soldier.

"The location of the stolen property," the policeman said. This was a question but he said it as if it were a statement.

Rising on his toes, Grocia peered around the yard looking for help. "Please tell these men I am not a thief," he called to the crowd.

A rifle butt crushed his foot and he collapsed.

"God help us," my mother said.

I prayed someone would say something, convince these men that our neighbor did not deserve to be hurt further. I prayed that all the soldiers and police would leave the yard now. I wished it were another day, a day when we played games and chased one another, and I went to Ceder to learn. Closing my eyes, I tried to tell myself it was all just a nightmare.

When I opened my eyes, the soldier in the brown uniform had a lock cutter in one hand, its handles as long as his arms and the blades curved like the pointed claw of an angry monster. My mother turned away.

"We punish thieves," the soldier said, using Polish for the first time. He swung the lock cutter open and pressed the open blades against Grocia's face, around his nose.

His comrades clasped Grocia's shoulders, while other soldiers held his wife at arm's length.

"Anything?" the soldier asked.

Without waiting, he scissored the lock cutter closed, hammering the handles against one another.

Blood shot from Grocia's face, his nose attached now

by only a small flap of skin near his eyes. He shuddered and whipped his head in agony. The soldiers dropped him and he crumpled to the ground. His nose lay next to him in a pool of blood.

One of Grocia's children screeched, the others looking on with a silent glare that told me everything they were feeling. His wife dropped to her knees. Grocia's body shuddered in a way I had never seen before.

"I want to go home now," I said to my father and Herzil.

God will not protect us, I thought. This made me feel breathless, ill.

But we are together, I told myself, studying my mother and father, my sisters crouching behind us on the street. I was so thankful for that. It seemed that nothing could take us away from each other.

Chapter 5

Neighborhood Services

Columbia Point, Boston
October 1961

Columbia Point, a neighborhood in Boston and a founder-
ing example of urban renewal gone wrong, had no trees.
Walking there for the first time, that was what struck
me; that was what I muttered out loud to no one. "No
trees, but a sound that seems familiar." From the stark
brick high-rises stretching up twenty stories or so came
the low hum of a distraught community. Through open
windows I could hear the voices, the noises of life on the
edge of society. Babies wailing; adults arguing; an odd
clattering of pots and pans; doors slamming; and plain-
tive moaning, all merging together into a low rumble.

The sounds from the prison camp of Dachau rushed back at me. The groans and the weeping. Children begging. The hollow thuds of gunstocks against frail bodies. Again, a constant low growl of anguish to which no one paid attention.

I looked around. High-rise after high-rise. No parks here, no athletic fields, just one small store at the very end of the development. A rat the size of a cat ran from underneath the building closest to me, squirming through a partially broken door. There was only one road in and only one road out of Columbia Point, unless, I was told, you could swim a mile and a half to Carson Beach. "There weren't too many takers on that, either," the head of Neighborhood Services told me, smirking. "If they don't kill each other there, swimming in that polluted shit will kill them anyway."

Columbia Point is where they sent me on my first assignment. "It's a very tough place, not one you would want to visit, and most people don't," said the administrator to whom I would be reporting when he received me at the school, an odd resigned smile falling across his tired features. I realized this was kind of a joke that they played on the new guy whose accent was very hard to understand and who dressed differently from everyone else. "Truant officers have a shelf life of about three days at Columbia Point," he continued, "so don't worry about it. Get a coffee and a sandwich and go or don't. No one will know and in a few weeks we will try to get you another neighborhood."

"No, this will be fine," I said. "I have been trained for this." After the Holocaust ended, my family and friends were all gone, I had moved to Boston to try to make a new life for myself and earned a degree in psychology. This was my first job.

"There is no school that gets you prepared for this," he said.

"I wasn't referring to school," I said, rising to leave.

He looked at me suspiciously but with confusion also. I thought about telling him where I'd been, what I'd seen, and how I'd barely survived my childhood. I wanted to scream at him but instead I breathed, trying to stop the scars of my past from getting the better of me.

Pinia's face came back to me, sweet Pinia who told everyone I was smart and strong and who asked me to remember him after he was gone. My stomach tightened. There were the piles of bodies pushed into mass graves and either covered or incinerated. There were the rapes and the molestations; the fighting over cups of dirty brown soup or a sliver of a potato. Beatings and fear. The trains from one camp to the next. The smells, the sounds, the unimaginable evil.

I stared at this man from Neighborhood Services and remembered more.

There were the tears streaming down the cheeks of the American soldiers liberating us at Dachau, unsure their own eyes were not deceiving them as they pushed their way deeper into the camp. There were the hours and days of wandering, a child hoping beyond hope that he would find his parents, his family. There was the hospital for war orphans, overrun and frightening, me hoarding food, hiding it under my bed and in my small locker, a glass of milk more precious than anything I'd known in my short life. There was the boy in the bed next to mine, the Nazi Youth swastika tattooed on his arm, a grim expression on his face whenever I dared to look over. Would he try to kill me in my sleep? They said I was finally safe, but was I?

I told the administrator I was pleased with the assignment and was on my way. Heading toward my mission, heading toward Columbia Point, I gathered myself, focused on how I came to be where I was at that moment and how I could use what I'd learned to help the lives of those in this neighborhood.

Images of the boat to America, crowded and fraught with uncertainty, every face scared and hopeful at once, floated into in my memory. The grim stare of the officer at Ellis Island who declared I was no longer Szmulek, but was now Steve, stabbed at me and made me wince. The orphanage in Boston where I learned to speak English, and the school for kids like me in Windsor, in western Massachusetts, where they sent me to learn a trade: Could I use these experiences to help the kids in Columbia Point? My friend Berger told me again and again that education was everything until I finally listened and took my studies seriously. Could these kids I was about to mentor come to feel the same way? Could I convince them that sleeping in the backseat of the rattletrap car I bought after pumping gas all summer near my college so I would be sure never to miss a class had been worth it?

Could Columbia Point be worse than where I'd been and what I'd seen? Could it be worse than starving and being abused and beaten, and seeing everyone you loved torn away and taken to their deaths? I had weighed less than eighty pounds when the soldiers came to Dachau.

The headmaster at the William E. Russell School, near Columbia Point, brought me into his office and explained that I was the fifth truant officer to come this year.

"Almost thirty percent of the students are absent today," he said. "There are the names." He handed me a list.

"Where are all the students?" I asked, shocked at what I was seeing.

"Who knows? Maybe smoking dope, or beating someone up. I don't know. All I know is that they are not here where they are supposed to be." With his sleeve, he wiped the sweat from his brow, his blue shirt turning damp from elbow to wrist.

I tried not to stare, but I'm sure my mouth was gaping. I was appalled by the man's callousness.

Chapter 6

A Safe Way Out

Krasnik
Autumn 1939

For the remainder of the night and throughout the next day, my father prayed and seemed lost in thought. Mumbling passages and whispering to himself, in both Yiddish and Polish, he rocked in his chair, eyes closed, his hands in constant motion rubbing his arms as if he was trying to stay warm. Tears came intermittently, also, followed always by trembling, and nothing, not my mother's gentle hand on his back or her soft words in his ear, seemed to calm his concerns.

"The Torah," he said intermittently. "We must protect the Torah."

When a moonless darkness fell over the yard, I heard the door open and close and after taking stock, I realized Herzil had left the apartment. I had no idea where he was headed or why he thought it was safe to wander out where so much terror had occurred, but I was certain that he had a reason and marveled at his bravery. Could I possibly have such courage, I wondered. He was, after all, older and stronger. I was only eight. I promised myself that I could be brave, but also that I would never leave my parents for very long. I couldn't. I loved them too much.

Stretching on my toes, I tried to peer down and see if I could follow Herzil through the dimness. Babsa pulled me back from the window.

"These monsters will shoot you if they see you, Szmulek," she said. "Stay out of sight."

I slept little that first night following the invasion of our yard, imagining terrible tortures being administered to Herzil and recalling the afternoon's horrors. Still, at dawn I again took to the window, ignoring Babsa's warning, hoping to see my brother racing back home or, by divine miracle, some indication that our ordeal was over. Instead Grocia's blood continued to empty in rivers toward Kammiena #3, and debris from Gramma Jietta's chair was scattered across the yard where days before I had played with Pinia. My hearted pounded. I questioned whether I'd ever see Pinia again; whether we'd ever again run in the yard.

Without asking—and knowing I'd be scolded—at dusk I slipped out of the apartment. I descended the stairs as quickly as I could, ignoring open doors, praying my footfalls would go undetected; and crouching to stay out of sight, I stepped across the yard and only then started to run. I had to help my father. He needed someone to answer his questions. He needed to know that the Torah at the synagogue was safe; that when he returned to pray, the scrolls would be there, still in the ark, still covered by the parocheth, still the word of God.

Hiding in an alley, I dodged a patrol of German soldiers marching down Kammiena #3, and after they passed I raced up Pilzuski Street. Breathless, I reached the steps of Aron Kodesh Shul, and leaping two steps at a time I climbed toward the arched entrance. My stomach turned: The doors were shattered. One set of hinges was broken completely from the frame; the other held only shards of wood. Sledgehammered pieces lay everywhere.

I thought about my father. "Papa," I said to no one.

Quivering with fear, I ascended the last steps, moving slowly and quietly, my breathing making more noise than I thought possible. Would whoever did this still be inside? Would they kill me for being there?

I peered inside and nearly gagged. A stench pushed me backward two steps and I teetered on the top stair, almost tumbling before catching my balance. Shit and piss were everywhere. Puddles in the aisles; brown and black heaps on the bimah; stains on the walls. What little light there was came from broken windows and illuminated the mess: the rabbi's chair shattered, Sabbath candlesticks soaking in a urine pool, the ark open and empty. My heart sank. The Torah. Torn and crumpled across one aisle and unraveled down another; the soldiers had taken every opportunity to desecrate it. I could practically see them stomping on it with joy, unbuttoning their pants, squatting over it, laughing.

"Papa cannot see this," I said. I wished Herzil was with me, certain he would know how to clean the scroll, make it the way it was, make Papa happy. I picked up a torn end and the paper disintegrated into yellowish mush. Were there other pieces I could save? I cried. It was as if they had murdered it, like they'd killed Grocia and the others, taking joy in what they did. Papa will weep and weep when he hears of this, I thought. I worried his heart might actually give out, and a paralyzing fear circulated through me.

As fast as my legs would carry me, I ran home.

"Szmulek," my mother screamed. "Oh, Szmulek. Oh, Szmulek. I thought you were dead."

My father was dovening in the corner.

"Where were you? Why did you leave? Where did you go?"

Babsa was crying also.

I hugged my mother, reaching around her waist, burying my face in the folds of her dress.

"Szmulek, where were you," she whispered. I could hear her sniffing the air around me. I was certain, somehow, she knew what had happened from the odor now permeating my clothes. My eyes were filled with tears when I turned to look at her. She wiped my cheeks with her thumbs. "My sweet boy," she said. "My sweet, sweet boy.

"Josef," she said firmly, staring now at my father. "Tomorrow, we are leaving here. It is no longer safe for us to stay."

Not long after dark Herzil returned, and with him were my nieces and nephews, my sisters and their husbands. Square black suitcases, overstuffed and looking as if they would burst open and spill their contents across the floor, were propped against the door as my relatives shuffled inside. Our already crowded apartment seemed hopelessly inadequate.

"Did you bring food?" my mother asked.

"There is some bread, and some Swiss cheese," Abe, Mala's husband, said. He was a squat man with a warm smile and a soft voice. "But soldiers came and took the rest. The police helped them."

Herzil and my mother moved to a corner and whispered, but I could hear them.

"I have arranged for a farmer to take us to Krasnik," Herzil said. "He has a horse and a cart and has agreed to stay with us until we reach the border of Russia. We can cross there. Three days it should take us. We will not be able to carry everything."

"We will be safe in Russia?" my mother asked.

"Once we get across we'll be safe."

My mother did not seem convinced. Her shoulders slumped and her eyes narrowed. She looked tired and this made me worry.

In the corner my nieces and nephews had climbed onto my father's lap, and he stroked their faces and hair. He tried to smile but tears overwhelmed him. He put them down, one at a time, stood, and faced the wall, his hands outstretched as if he were hugging the apartment. His body shook. His arms trembled. His legs looked as if they would soon give way. We all studied his agony.

He stopped and turned, wiping his tears with his sleeve.

A pleasant ring radiated from the pocket of his vest and this noise seem to wake him. With eyes wide and clear, for several moments he did not move. He wore a look as if he were hearing this sound for the first time, and as if the chime itself was calling to him.

"Herzil," he said, rummaging through his pockets. "Herzil, come here." Lifting the watch from his vest, he ran his fingers along the tiny chain that led to his belt. He unhooked it. "Herzil," he said. "You must take this. It is old and valuable."

"No, Papa," Herzil said, turning back to my mother. He waved at the air as if he wanted to hear nothing further.

"This was my father's, your grandfather's. The watchmaker has fixed it a thousand times and it is still keeping time. You must take it."

"No."

"But where I am going, Herzil, I will not need it." Opening Herzil's hand, he placed the watch on his palm, then closed my brother's fingers around it.

"We are all going together, Papa," Herzil said, pulling away. "We are all going to Russia together to start a new life."

My father went back to his chair. He began to pray again.

"Tomorrow morning," Herzil announced to everyone. "We are going to Russia. Pack your things."

The line of families leaving Lodz, to my eyes, seemed endless. Families, large and small, some pushing carts by hand, others carrying loads wrapped in cloth sacks tied around their shoulders, trudged forward but at a pace that seemed to me too slow to get anywhere. We had a horse, at least the farmer did whom Herzil had paid to take us to the Russian border, but the animal was old and crooked and walked with a limp. I wasn't sure how far it could go.

By midmorning we had left the city behind and the line thinned as some families turned north, others west, and still others turned around and returned home. We headed east along with many who'd heard that Russia was a safe haven for Jewish families, and as I listened while I walked, I overheard many conversations about how life was going to be different; about how food was going to be plentiful; and about how beautiful Ukraine was; most concluding: Weren't we lucky to be going there. While I hoped it was true and that my father would again need his pocket watch, I began to wonder, if Russia was so wonderful, why hadn't we gone there before. I also noticed with dread that people began to abandon their suitcases, leaving them open and half full at the side of the road as they realized that their loads were too heavy to carry all the way to the peace and good fortune ahead.

All that night we walked, though for a few hours I slept in the cart, lying between two suitcases, using Herzil's coat as a pillow. My nieces and nephews were in the cart with me as well, and though my mother said if we huddled together we'd be more likely to stay warm, none of us could get comfortable, so we spread ourselves around and tried not to complain. Autumn cold had come, especially at night, and by the time I woke my toes felt frozen, my hands ached, and my nose and lips felt chafed and cracked. My mother tried to give me her shawl to warm me but I could see she was freezing herself and more than tired. "I don't need it," I said. Standing on the wood frame of the cart I put it back around her.

Morning brought our progress to a crawl. The farmer needed to let his horse rest and eat, and Herzil dispensed small pieces of bread and cheese—both of which seemed so old and stale their flavor had simply vanished. The scraps must have been spoiled as Anka went pale and had to run into the trees several times to vomit and go to the bathroom, leaving us waiting by the side of the road. Ashen and grim-faced, and obviously in pain, she began to cough and wheeze when she returned to us. Even through her exhaustion, my mother looked terrified at Anka's symptoms.

German patrols also passed us every few miles and though some ignored us, most made us stop, rifled through the cart, and barked questions none of us but the farmer could understand. He answered all their questions correctly, or so it seemed to me, since every time he responded, he and the soldiers laughed and patted each other on the shoulders, after which we were permitted to move on. "*Juden*," I often heard them say to one another before they let us go. And sometimes they watched us for long periods as we moved into the distance, guns slung over their shoulders, their bayonets stabbing at the sky. They scared me the way they followed us with their eyes. Their faces said: They don't know where they are going.

By the second evening Herzil, too, was coughing, and his breathing became noisy and sounded painful. Both my mother and father begged him to stop and rest and take some tea, but without talking he waved away their concerns and we plodded on. I watched him carefully, and saw that he spent an hour shivering followed by an hour when he seemed too hot to wear any clothes, sweat pouring from his forehead, his shirt soaked through. "It's typhus," he said to my mother, covering his mouth with a rag. "I'll find medicine when we get to Krasnik."

"For Anka also," my mother said.

"For Anka also," Herzil replied.

When the sun came up and we'd stopped again to rest the horse, my sisters rummaged through the cart, finally announcing that we had no more food. My father cried and prayed to God to help us, and one of my nephews began to cry as well, but Herzil announced we were close to Russia and that we'd all have more than we could imagine in just a few hours. The farmer rolled his eyes at Herzil when he made his pronouncement and I knew this meant we still had far to travel, but as no one else had seen him I decided to stay quiet. "Mama, we will be there soon," I said, taking her hand.

She nodded and we both watched the farmer reach into his saddlebag. He lifted a folded cloth from inside, a faint smell of meat drifting back to us. Sensing that we were watching him, he turned, shrugged, and unpeeled a slab of pork from the cloth, ignoring us. As he tore at it with his teeth, shreds fell to the ground.

I'd never had pork, knew it was forbidden and probably as filthy as I had been told a thousand times, but my mouth watered and my breathing quickened.

"No, Szmulek," my mother said, squeezing my hand. "There will be something to eat soon."

Hunger tore at us but when the sun rose on the fifth

day of our travels, in the distance we could see the roof-tops of Krasnik. Excitement seemed to give us energy even though it had been days since we had eaten, and even Anka and Herzil, both of whom had grown too weak to walk, sat up in the cart and smiled at our good fortune. Now we could go to Russia. Now we would find food. I imagined a new and shiny butcher shop my father could operate. I thought about Herzil getting well and carrying me on his back. I hoped I'd find a new seder so I could learn to pray like my father.

"Szmulek, be careful," Abe called out to me. My imaginings dissolved and I realized I had drifted into the middle of the road. Stepping aside, I stopped and stared at a long line of families going the opposite way. I glanced at Abe, and both of us frowned. We were all thinking the same thought. Beside me now, my mother seemed frightened.

We were weak and tired and hungry, but these people were weighted down with something more; stooped and hobbled; lost and hopeless; grim and pale.

"You're going the wrong way," Abe said, loudly, though his words faded as he came to the end of his sentence.

No one spoke and only a few lifted their eyes and bothered to acknowledge that we were there.

The line stretched back as far as I could see.

Krasnik was much smaller than Lodz, at least that is what I was told—but to me it seemed much more crowded and fraught with apprehension. Everyone, it appeared, milled about in the streets; some racing nervously past us, frantically checking behind them as if they were being chased; others, their heads down in despair, trudging aimlessly, glancing at us when they dared, but warily. Soldiers, too, filled the blocks and the yards, pointing this direction and that, shouting orders at people and families. Their faces all looked menacing and stern when I managed to raise the courage to look at them. They seemed, with their expressions, to warn anyone who passed not to stop or otherwise get in their way.

Rain came by midmorning, and though my mother and Abe discussed continuing on and heading directly to the border, the weather and the worsening illnesses of Herzil and Anka made them decide to try to find shelter. Abe blocked people in the street, making them stop and questioning them as to where we might find refuge from the conditions, but few seemed interested in our problem and some darted away in fright when he mentioned "typhus." My mother also asked passersby if they could help us, mostly approaching women who looked friendly or who stared at the soldiers with defiance. Silence or an indifferent shrug was mostly what she received in return for her inquiries.

I was certain we'd be left without help and forced to spend another night in hunger—while I watched them both plead for assistance—but as the rain gave way to a chilling wind, a woman, stooped and frail, stared at our cart and our shivering faces and pointed down an alley. My mother and Abe kissed her, my mother holding the woman's hand to her lips, tears of gratitude flowing down her cheeks. "Go, go, go," the woman said to my mother. "Get those children out of this cold."

The alley led us to a synagogue, or at least a building that used to be a synagogue. A Star of David was etched into the wall above the doorway and square Hebrew lettering was printed upon the eaves, but inside the shul had been dismantled. There were no chairs or benches, the bimah was covered with piles of firewood and coal, and two stained-glass windows were shattered, sharp points of purple and green glass clawing at the air. Two horses and a mule were stabled in one corner, a family huddled nearby hoping to draw some of the animals' warmth. Many others slept or crowded into small circles across the floor. Suspicious looks followed us when we chose a small unoccupied area. An hour later the wariness turned to bitterness when Herzil and Anka continued to cough and gasp, the sounds of their illnesses seeming to echo throughout the building.

"Is it typhus?" someone called out.

"They are just tired," my mother called back.

I was frightened by the arguments that came next. Nearly everyone seemed to be shouting at us or at each other and several men approached and demanded that we leave at once, threatening to throw out the few items we had brought in from the cart and to toss us all out violently as well.

"Please," my mother begged. "We just need to rest. We have not slept or eaten."

"You must take them to Janf Lubelski at once," a woman shouted. "The hospital there will care for them."

My mother nodded slowly and looked around for help. Abe was gone, out searching on a rumor he'd heard about trains into Ukraine. My sisters were all sleeping, children tucked in around them. My father was praying, standing in the corner, begging God to make his son and daughter well, rubbing his tallits, staring upward as if he might, if he peered hard enough, get a glimpse of the creator. Herzil and Anka were covered by our only blanket. They were both shivering.

"I can help you, Mama," I said.

"Finish the soup, Szmulek," she replied. A woman in little more than rags had brought me a bowl of cold broth with a single carrot floating near the surface. Why I deserved the soup I had no idea but I sipped it and felt the dull saltiness slide down my throat.

"Mama, I will share with you," I said.

"Leave some for your sisters if you can," she replied.

"I will," I said. "They can have the rest." I gave her the

bowl, but my eyes must have betrayed me. I was so hungry. My heart raced and I realized I was shaking.

"Shh," my mother said, hugging me close. "It's all right now. Shh."

I quickly fell asleep.

Janf Lubelski was less than a day's walk from Krasnik and the small clinic there did not care that we were Jews. I waited outside for my mother, worrying that someone else in my family might come down with this sickness, certain suddenly that it might be my mother or father, and panic shot through me. What if my mother never came out? What if the doctors inside made her stay with Anka and we weren't allowed to return to Krasnik? What would happen to my sisters and me, our father, to my nieces and nephews? Soldiers might come, Germans.

My mother did eventually come out, hugged me, and calmed me enough to share the half potato and bread slice she carried with her, a gift from a nurse inside who saw me crying on the steps.

She'd informed me that my brother and sister would remain there for several days and that we had to return to the others.

I nodded and squeezed her hand tighter. "Perhaps Abe has found some food," I said.

First, though, we would need to gather our strength.

We found an alley snaking to an obscure exit of the hospital, and there we curled up around each other and for perhaps an hour we slept—me leaning against my mother, her arms wrapped around my shoulders.

Then we rose again, stomachs rumbling. The night was dark and clear and cool and so we began to walk. Patrols seemed to be everywhere, on foot, in trucks, and even some on horseback, and again we were stopped often and questioned.

"Juden?" they again asked my mother, in German.

Pushing me behind her to protect me, she responded using what little German she knew, rambling slightly until they grew tired and moved on. I held my breath each time they approached us. As soon as they departed, longs sighs of relief came from both our lungs.

"The synagogue is warm, and perhaps there will be another bowl of soup," she said, smiling, when one group of soldiers walked away.

"I hope so," I said.

My legs were stiff and sore and my feet ached as well by the time we found ourselves at the outskirts of Krasnik. We smiled at one another, glad our journey was nearly over, but we both could sense that there was more trouble ahead. An anxious silence came between us while we walked. When we reached the synagogue again, my mother fell to her knees.

The doors had been bolted and a sign hung with nails.

"What does it say?" I asked. "What does the sign say?" I was certain it was for us; that it said my entire family was gone, taken to prison, beaten, lit on fire, or had their noses cut off.

"It says: CONDEMNED. NO ONE ALLOWED INSIDE," Abe said from behind us. My mother jumped to her feet and hugged him. "The local authorities are going to be treating the building with chemicals," he continued. "They knew Herzil and Anka had typhus. We all had to leave."

"The other families," my mother said. "They had nowhere to go."

Abe paused and seemed to decide that we didn't need to know how mad people were. "We're safe now," Abe said. "Come, we found a room. For a while we will have to make the best of it."

"Szmulek, put this on," my mother said. We needed to go now.

"I'm not cold, Mama," I said.

"You will need the pockets," she replied.

I did not understand her. "Where are we going, Mama?"

"The train station," she said.

"Is Papa there? Are we going to get Herzil and Anka?"

"No," she said. "No more questions."

Obeying her, I walked as fast as I could, trying not to slow us down. The sun had fallen below the horizon, leaving only gray light behind, but I could see my mother study everyone who passed us, warily looking for something or someone that might interrupt whatever it was we were doing. German patrols crossed our path and she frowned and made low noises. Others—families, residents, and vendors—she sneered at suspiciously. Our pace quickened.

Nearing the station, we turned down an alley. Night had fallen and oil lamps from the main road faded into the distance behind us. A train whistle sounded and my mother stopped and looked panicked. We stood and listened until it eventually dissolved into the air. As soon it was gone we continued walking.

Dodging in and out between buildings and peering around corners to be certain we were undetected, we finally emerged into a field across from the station. Crouching, we were still and quiet. Trains were lined up in rows, bending with the tracks, snaking out in both directions. Opposite us, on the other side of the trains, the station house lights shimmered and glowed. Freight cars blocked our view of the platform so we could not see if anyone was there, but we heard no noise.

One finger to her lips, my mother gestured to remain quiet. Staying low, we crossed the first track between two cars that were uncoupled, then the next track as well. As we scurried from one car to the next, Mama lifted me so I could peer inside. We were searching for food. We needed to steal food to survive.

"It's empty, Mama," I whispered. "This one, too."

Most of the cars had been unloaded, leaving only dust and hay and heavy dank air. Some had steel bars or wood piled in the corners. In one, a cow chewed on grasses from a bin at its front feet, a chain running around its neck attached to a large hook hanging from the ceiling.

"There is no food here, Mama," I said.

"There is," she replied so softly I could barely hear her.

We crossed over another set of tracks, crawling this time, the flatbed cars providing little cover. My hands and feet hurt, but I was certain this was more difficult for my mother. Low groans came from the back of her throat while we inched along the stone bed. When we finally stood with our backs pinned against the freight cars of the next train, she started to cry softly.

"I'm sorry, Szmulek," she murmured.

"Mama," I said, peeking through the door, which was ajar. "Mama, look."

She turned and stared inside with me. Potato and onion bins and pickle barrels filled half the car. Turnips and apples were heaped against the far wall. Neither of us spoke. Our good fortune was more than we could express. Papa will be so happy, I thought. Everyone will be so happy. We will never be hungry again.

With a boost, my mother pushed me up and I squeezed through the partially opened door. Almost shaking with excitement, I danced from bin to bin, smelling the light, sweet aromas, grabbing a pickle and swallowing it in three bites. A potato was next and I didn't care that it was raw or still dusty with dirt. Cool and milky when I pierced the skin with my teeth, I chewed the meat until it dripped from my lips onto my sweater.

"Fill your pockets, Szmulek," I heard my mother mutter. "Take as much as you can. Hurry."

"Shall I hand you down some potatoes?"

She did not respond.

"Mama?"

No answer came.

My pulse raced. Where had she gone?

Footsteps crunching the stones on the track bed made me suddenly understand. To me it sounded like a thousand men, their boots crushing the gravel beneath their feet, their voices amplified, their guns rattling against their sides with each step. I backed into the corner, cowering behind a barrel, quietly pulling loose hay up around me. They spoke German. I could hear their words and accents. My mother was going to be killed. And then they would find me. I did not breathe.

They passed.

I remained still as their voices trailed off and disappeared in the distance. Quiet filled the air for ten minutes before I stirred. What if they came back? What if they brought dogs to smell us? What if my mother had run away and been captured and beaten? What if she was dead? What would I do? I felt like crying but didn't.

Wedging myself out the door, I climbed down and rolled under the train to hide, lying on the stones. I was so tired. I was so scared. I wanted to go back to Lodz, back to our apartment, back to meals of kapusniak, back to the bakery, back to seder, back to when my father took me to shul. I didn't want to steal anymore. I didn't want to hide. I didn't want any of this. I wanted to go home.

"Szmulek?"

"Mama?"

A leg, and then two came down from under the carriage of the train. Grasping the axle, she lowered herself and sat beside me.

"You can balance on the casing above the axle, Szmulek," she said, as if stunned she had survived. "You can balance on the casing above the axle," she repeated as if even she didn't believe it. She stared at it.

Scrambling into her lap, I wrapped my arms around her neck and buried my face into her shoulder. We both wept, and she rocked in place as she rubbed my back and kissed my forehead.

"I want to go home now," I whispered.

"In just a few minutes," she replied quietly. She pulled my face up so I could see her grim smile. "First, let's take as much as we can carry."

Chapter 7

A Friend in Boston

Columbia Point, Boston
October 1961

A concentration camp it wasn't, but Columbia Point held dangers that were indeed many and unrelenting. Gangs ruled portions of the Point, Boston's ghetto—with affiliations that spread out across the more dilapidated parts of the city—selling drugs, coaxing girls into prostitution, and terrorizing businesses and those who weren't "in." The one road passing across the Point was also menacing. Huge trucks, some headed to the city dump next door, sped by without caution or care, and because there was no fence or barrier children were constantly dodging in and out of oblivious traffic. Hit-and-runs were common and even when two, then three, then four children died, the city did nothing. These were the forgotten people, and few of these deaths were even investigated. "They get housing—tell them to watch their own kids," a cop told me early in my tenure. "What do you care?"

I cared because I saw unemployment in a vicious cycle with crime and violence; I cared because I saw alcohol and drug abuse tearing families apart; I cared because dozens of Columbia Point's young people were not attending school on a regular basis, or at all, and it was both my job and my intention to get them back in school. For how would they escape this if not with the help of people like me and their teachers? Their lives may not have been as bleak as mine once was, but after the Holocaust ended I had lifelines they didn't. There was no orphanage or hospital or trip to America to save them.

I decided I had to use a nontraditional but straightforward approach to getting the students back to school, an approach I was sure no one had tried before. I took the truancy list and began to knock on the doors of all the students who had not attended school. As I trudged through the Point, crisscrossing from building to building, wary eyes were always on me. Passersby stared or did double takes when I nodded, greeting them. Men gathered in groups glared at me, wondering, I'm sure, who this odd man with a clutch of papers was and what he was doing in their neighborhood.

"How did you make it this far without getting the shit kicked out of you?" a woman said to me, her door open only a crack. I presented her with my truancy officer identification—a gesture that had resulted in several doors being slammed in my face that morning—and she studied it, confused, before letting the door open a bit wider. "What do you want?" she asked.

"It is not the easiest thing to speak to someone through a nearly closed door," I said.

She laughed, and for some reason I was laughing right along with her.

The door was open now.

"Well, you don't look like the police. If you are, we are all in trouble," she said, gauging me. "So what is with the clothes?" She led me into her apartment, which was gleaming and immaculate. I sensed that a woman who took that much pride in her surroundings would also take great pride in her children. "Now what brings you here today to my door?" she asked.

A cup of coffee and a plate of bacon and something resembling oatmeal appeared on the table, and with an open hand she offered me a chair.

The food looked delicious, and I stared at it. Memories of hunger, of longing for any morsel of food that might save me from starving, made me pause. This gesture from a stranger confused me for a moment. I don't know how long I studied the plate.

"People eat food all the time," she said. "It isn't poison or anything."

I finally looked up at her and smiled.

"Hmm, food got you speechless," she said, watching me curiously. "Please, please. Sit down. Try it."

Five forkfuls in, I smiled.

"That's quite a grin," she said. "Penny for your thoughts."

"I was just thinking that here is a Polish Jew sitting in a young Irish woman's kitchen having a chat and some food. Only in America."

She was staring at my tattoo, 148127. She seemed distraught. "Were...were you one of those people? In one of those camps the Germans made? Those places they..."

"Yes, I was there," I said, glancing at my arm. "I was a boy."

"And you survived all that?"

"Yes. I was lucky."

"Hm, lucky, okay. You eat as much as you want. And there is more, too."

"Thank you," I said. I put my fork down. "I am here, though, about your daughter."

"Maureen? Why are you here about Maureen?"

Wiping my mouth with the napkin she passed to me, I could see from her expression that she had no idea what her child had been up to. "She doesn't go to school. The school hasn't seen her in weeks."

"I don't understand. She got dressed in her school

dress and had all her books when she left this morning. She does that every morning. Why would she be skipping school?"

I decided not to speak, to let what I was saying make its way through her thoughts.

"And she comes home and says school was fine...and tells me..." Her head was bowed. "My Maureen doesn't go to school."

I nodded, then waited.

"So where does she go?" A stern glare fell across her features.

I shrugged. "I'm sorry, I don't know, but not to school. Apparently, this has been going on for months."

"So why are you just coming now to tell me?"

"I just started yesterday," I said. "I am trying to see all the parents of kids who don't attend. A lot don't want to see me. At a lot of places, it seems like no one is home."

Tears filled her eyes. "You think I'm a terrible parent?"

"I do not think that," I said. "If you had known sooner, you would have done something. I can see that."

"I don't understand why, if they've known about this for months, I am just hearing about it."

Silence filled the space between us. I shrugged. "The man from Neighborhood Services told me no one wanted this job."

"But you do?"

"I've seen so many lives wasted. So many more than I

could ever count. So many children. If I can try to keep that from happening, why isn't that a job that anyone would want? I'm not going to be a tycoon, right. Look at me. My accent. This is better anyway. This is real work."

Staring at me, she smiled. "Maureen will be in school tomorrow. I can promise you that," she said.

"Good," I said. "Thank you for that."

She shook her head. "Thanking me?... You're amazing. Maybe a little crazy to be out here, but God bless you."

And with that she rose and hugged me, then kissed me on the cheek.

Chapter 8

The Farm

Krasnik
Winter 1940

Winter set in upon us with bleak frozen winds and gray skies that hung low over Krasnik and never seemed to move. Snow fell often, piling against our building, and tiny icy tornadoes blew off the drifts, swirling over the pond behind us until they disappeared, swept away by more powerful gusts. The cold tested us. How much could our family endure? We were frightened all the time and seemed always to be waiting for the Germans to burst through the door, screaming at us, threatening us, to tell us we could no longer stay in our room. The frigid temperatures would have made that deadly.

Herzil and Anka, especially, wouldn't last long outside. They had returned but were both so weak, standing was difficult and sleep seemed to provide their only peace. If the Germans came now, surely they would die. But the rest of us, too, would be in terrible danger. We lacked warm clothing and food and had nowhere else to go. Our shoes were tattered—practically worn through—and our supply of wood to make a fire was pitifully small. Babsa was making it plain she would go no farther.

Our room seemed numb as well. I could recall the smell of soup or cabbage cooking on our stove in Lodz, but here there was only the odor of dampness and mildew. Ice bulged in from cracks in the walls and ceiling, and the lone window was so caked with frozen dirt and lodged snow, only a vague translucent light illuminated our space. Sounds were scarce also, adding to the dormancy. Other than my father's droning prayers, only the monotonous rhythm of our breathing broke the silence—a gray vapor mist trailing each exhale before disappearing into the cold night.

Sleep seemed to be our most regular habit. Weak from so little food, we huddled together under one of the few blankets that wasn't torn or wet, dreams of better times and places coming easily and often. I liked it when I heard my sisters softly snoring or saw my mother's eyes grow heavy and finally close. I was certain they were off somewhere, eating feasts and dancing, lighting the candles on the Sabbath or basking in warm sunshine. I imagined them singing and laughing and playing with my nieces and nephews. They were happy. There was joy.

Someone stirred and coughed, and I realized my nose was freezing.

"Abe," Herzil whispered, gripping Abe's sleeve. "They are building labor camps, now. There was talk at the hospital."

"I know," Abe said. "I know."

"What is this thing, a labor camp?" my mother asked. She was lying across the room at Abe's feet. She leaned on an elbow and stared at them. Peering around the room, she checked to see if I was awake. I pretended I was not.

The first whisperings were spreading that the Germans were rounding up Jews and forcing them into camps, working them like slaves building guns and trucks and bombs, many until they died.

The lines of ragged people trudging to the train station suddenly made sense. Hundreds had passed through our area carrying suitcases, surrounded by German soldiers prodding them on with the butts of their weapons, their boots, or their fists. They were lifeless, some crying, others flushed with hunger.

I thought about my friend Pinia. I was certain I'd find him in Russia when we got there, and that he'd tell me again that I was smart and brave, and make me feel important and proud. I'd convinced myself he'd be with me soon, and his voice resonated in my imagination. *This*

is Szmulek, and when he grows up he will do things to make
your life better. I am his good friend and I already know this
is true.

Pinia's family, they've gone over the border by now and
been taken in by a nice family, given shelter and food, I
mused. I'd see him again, as soon as we could go across.
I pictured him singing like he always did, running and
humming, and making up words as he played. I liked that
he always smiled, and I loved that he thought we'd always
be together.

"They don't take children, Mama," Herzil said. He was
pleading with her. "Do you understand? They don't take
children."

"I don't understand," my mother said. "No, I don't
understand you."

"Yes, you do," Herzil said.

My father was praying, mumbling in the corner.

"Josef," my mother said.

He did not stop to listen to her.

I squeezed my eyes shut. I tried desperately to remember all the families I had seen being pushed along toward
the station. Picturing the lines, I scanned up and down,
darting from person to person in my imagination. There
were no kids. I realized it now. No children. Where had
they gone? I was spinning with fear. I saw myself being
dragged away from my mother, both of us crying and

reaching for one another. Around me, other children were being pulled from their families, screaming and wailing, fingers touching until they were too far apart but still stretching, trying to hold on.

I was crying but I tried not to let anyone hear me.

"They will find us soon," Herzil said.

"We cannot let them find us," Abe said. "We have to try to cross the border again."

"Everyone has tried," Herzil said. "The border is closed. You know that."

"But Szmulek," my mother whispered. "*He* must go there. He must."

Footsteps and voices outside quieted everyone. Could this be the Germans? Would they come crashing through the door, murderous, snarling?

"Let them in," Abe said. "It's the girls."

Wind blew wisps of snow inside that settled on the floor and blankets as soon as the door closed behind my sisters. Anka was crying.

"We have bread, Mama," Anka said. "And two onions."

No one responded.

"We have bread for everyone," Anka repeated, her voice quivering. "Enough for everyone. Please, everyone, come eat now." She seemed unsteady.

Collapsing next to my mother, Anka covered her face with her hands and sobbed.

"Anka," my mother said. She spoke as if she wanted to question her but did not dare. "Anka," she repeated. "But…"

"We are starving to death," Anka said, tears falling now over her cheeks. "All of us."

I was only eight but I knew what this meant. They had lain down with men, strangers, and let them touch them for food. Our desperation had reached the point where everything we had ever learned meant nothing, even the word of God. Do not steal. Do not lie. These were all just words, written on some paper somewhere where people weren't starving and cold and sick and tired. What was right and what was wrong didn't matter, and I was so hungry I didn't really care.

Something had broken inside my father—his focus gone, his awareness waning, his life ebbing away. He was no longer the man who had taken me to shul, and to the seder, and to his butcher shop. That man was gone and I missed him. I longed for his stories and for his touch. I worried that he didn't even know me, or my mother, or my sisters. I didn't know why but I knew he was doomed. For a moment, I thought we all were.

"I will take Szmulek tomorrow," my mother said, hugging Mala and caressing her hair. "You're right. We can't wait any longer."

All the air left my lungs and blood pounded in my ears. I didn't know what she meant but I knew that wherever she was thinking of taking me, I didn't want to go.

These people were my entire life; all I knew and all I ever wanted to know, they'd told me. What would I be without them? Who would I be? Why would I be? But something also told me that if she was taking me somewhere it was because she wanted me to be safe; she wanted to protect me from the Germans who would soon drag the family to some horrific camp. She didn't want me to see Anka die, or Herzil die, or everyone die. I was a child. I was to be saved.

"He will pass," Abe said. "His Polish is good. Tell him to speak no Yiddish, no Hebrew. Tell him no matter what anyone says to him, only Polish."

My mother nodded.

"Take his yarmulke," Herzil said. "He wears it under his hat sometimes."

"Tell him to forget he is Jewish," Babsa said. "Forget this forever."

My parents walked me outside the village, where they had spotted a farm couple plowing a field. There my mother begged for their help.

Turning, the woman looked to her husband behind her, hoping for guidance. He looked away, back to his plow. Their farm was small but even through the cold I could smell the dirt and the animals. Letting the air roll over my tongue, I hoped the scents could somehow fill my stomach. They didn't so I glanced around. I hoped to see bread cooling on a windowsill or soup steaming from a black kettle suspended over a fire. Instead, two boys wrapped in scarves and heavy woolen coats tended to a wooden fence in the distance. One looked back and stared and nudged his brother to tell him to pay attention to these strangers near their barn.

I turned to their house. Gray stones wedged together to form the walls made it appear sturdy and I imagined the inside as warm and dry. Smoke drifting in swirls from the chimney added to my daydreams, but the woman's hand squeezing my cheeks focused my attention. She inspected me, turning my head from side to side.

"He's filthy," she said.

"We have nowhere to wash," my mother replied. "Where we live, we cannot..."

"Send them on their way," the husband said, still staring at his plow.

"Please, just my boy. The Germans will come for us soon. Please let the boy stay here."

"I want to go back with you," I said to my mother softly.

"Hush," she said.

"You are Jews?" the woman asked.

My mother did not speak but nodded slowly.

"They will kill all of us if they find him here, if we are found to be hiding him."

The boys were both standing now, staring. One used a

shovel, resting his head on his hands intertwined around the end of the long wooden handle. The other smiled at me and shrugged. They were older than I was, I could tell that from their size, but the distance and their bulky clothing made it hard to determine exactly their ages. "Let him stay, Papa," the smiling boy called across the field.

"Have you seen the signs?" the father shouted back.

They quickly went back to their work.

We had walked all day, finding the property only as dusk cut short the light. My feet were wet and cold, and my hands ached from being blown with frosty winds since morning. Now my cheeks hurt also from where the woman had gripped my face. I tried to rub away the aches with the backs of my hands.

"There are signs everywhere," she said to my mother. "ACHTUNG, HIDING JEWS WILL RESULT IN SEVERE PUNISHMENT. That is what they say. They are posted on every concrete stanchion between here and Warsaw. They burn everything if you violate these rules. Then they shoot you." She glanced at her husband again. "They give rewards if you turn someone in."

"Pasha," the husband said, softening. "It's okay. Take them inside and give them something to eat. The miserable vicious bastards take what they want anyway. Hiding Jews or not. What is your name, boy?" he asked.

"His name is Szmulek," my mother answered.

"Does he have his own tongue," the farmer said gently.

"My name is Szmulek," I said. "I'm very hungry if you don't mind."

"Mama, how will I find you when the war is over?" I said to my mother the following morning. Standing at the fence leading to the road we'd traveled the day before, my mother crouched and studied my face. She ran her hands along my arms and shoulders, caressed my cheeks, and brushed my eyes with her thumbs.

"We will find each other, Szmulek," she said. "We will." Her eyes were flooded with tears. "You'll be safe now," she said, her voice nearly too quiet to hear. "We will find each other someday. I promise. I promise." She kissed my forehead. "I love you, Szmulek."

She stood, turned, and stepped away down the road as quickly as she could.

Rain began to fall. Some part of me knew that I would never see her again, though it would be years before I would admit that to myself.

Chapter 9

Grandpa

Word of the strange man with the odd accent spread around Columbia Point, and eventually more and more doors opened when I knocked. Over time at the William E. Russell School there were fewer absentees, the headmaster nodded his appreciation when he saw me in the halls, and occasionally a parent would find me in the yard or in the parking lot and ask me for help. The children also came to know me, and daily rituals became something some of them clung to.

Instead of carrying coffee with me in the morning I always waited outside one building where two brothers, Tommy and Cal, lived. Tommy was eight. Cal had just turned ten. They liked to run to the shop and get me a pour. They both had warm smiles and they teased me as much as they did each other. I gave them a dollar each day and they'd bring me back the change, but when they handed it to me they knew I'd tell them to keep it so long as they used it to buy food.

My little friend Tilly, who was seven, also came to see me each day, her eyes bright and her school binder secured in a string attached to her wrist. We walked from the corner where she met me to the doorway of the school, and she held my hand so tightly it made me wonder if she could let go at all. It was the expression on her face, though—always upbeat and excited—and shock of dark curls that made me sure she had lots of friends other than me. Still, hers was another door I decided to frequent, a door even more quiet than at Tommy and Cal's.

Neighborhood Services began to take notice of my inroads also, and while I remained busy at the Point I was assigned to other tough areas as well. Old Harbor and D Street in South Boston were projects that also housed the poor but there the problems were not so much about school as they were about violence. Drugs and crime were rampant but for most, once you reached adolescence, staying alive was a day-to-day concern. Talking to teenagers was different from talking to children. I had to be tough but understanding as well.

"Get the fuck out of my area, Grandpa," a lanky Irish

kid screamed at me when I approached him and several friends camped out behind a chain-link fence surrounding an empty lot near D Street. "I'll be so glad to cut you," he seethed at me as I continued to move toward them.

"I am not afraid of you," I said calmly.

They laughed.

"I'm not," I offered, and now I was laughing, too. "Where I've been you wouldn't have lasted one day."

"And where is that?" he said, pulling a switchblade from his back pocket and slinging it open. "That where you got that fucked-up accent?"

"I can just tell you I survived much worse than you can give out." I shrugged. "So, anyway, what are you doing here?"

They stared at one another and from their expressions I could see that they had no answer.

"Give that some thought," I said. "I'll be back tomorrow."

Over the next several weeks I returned to the lot a few times a day as kids began to gather there at odd hours wanting to hear my story. By word of mouth the audience grew, and each time I recited the tale of something else the Nazis had done to me and others, their faces contorted into incredulity.

At first, I did all the talking, until slowly stories began to come back at me. They told me about their abusive homes and life on the streets; how they had to fend for themselves and hated school because it seemed like there was no point. No one in their neighborhoods ever got out, went to college, got jobs, or did anything with their lives. Their only choice was to stick together, to do what they had to do to survive, and often that meant defending themselves. Others, they said, had guns. They just had knives and their fists.

"I am going to help you," I said.

"Nobody helps us," the leader said.

"You don't have to trust me now," I said, "but you will."

One morning, in the cold of February, Tommy and Cal didn't come to the doorway where I waited. The next day nothing as well, so I went to their apartment.

Before I knocked, I put my ear to the door. Shuffling feet and muffled voices were inside, whispers really, that I couldn't quite make out. With a gentle tap, I let whoever was home know I was there. I waited. And waited some more. I tapped on the door again and when no one came I called out to Tommy and Cal.

"We're okay, Mr. Ross," Cal finally answered without opening the door. "We'll see you tomorrow, okay?"

"I need you to let me in, please," I said. "Whatever is wrong, I can help you."

No response came but there was a hushed debate raging on the other side of the door.

"Boys, it's okay. Please let me in."

"They're not going to let us be together," Tommy called out to me.

"Who?" I asked. "What do you mean by that? Boys, you need to let me in. I promise to help you and I promise no one will keep you from being together. I won't let that happen."

The low hum of discussion, jumbled and garbled, vibrated the door where I'd again placed my ear. Finally, the knob turned, slowly at first, clanging back twice before determination and resignation won out. The door opened.

I was forced to take a step back. The smell of death filled my nostrils and sent my mind reeling—for a moment I was back in Dachau, Auschwitz, Unterriexingen. Burned into my consciousness and welling inside me was the odor of lifeless bodies, the scent of fluids seeping from orifices that no longer functioned, the aroma of flesh on the verge of decomposing.

The boys stared up at me. I gathered myself.

"Come with me now," I commanded them. "Stay right here in the hall."

I crept inside, put a handkerchief to my nose, and moved from room to room. Thoughts of the filthy barracks where the emaciated died each day rushed back to me. The piles of bodies, bones and limbs protruding, being readied for the ovens, blinded me even as I walked. Rotting blood on the ground in pools came at me in flashbacks. Still, I continued, scanning as I went. I examined the cluttered kitchen, then the bathroom, then the main room, but kept moving. Turning to the bedroom, I knew what I'd see. Wrapped in a tattered blanket, a gray corpse rested on a top quilt. Her eyes were open, her hair pulled back away from her face. Her expression was one I was far too familiar with.

"They won't let us stay together," Tommy said again when I went back in the hall.

I knelt at their feet and took each by the hand. "You will be getting me coffee every day, together, for a very long time," I said. "Look at me." They did. "I lost my parents, too, when I was your age. I know what it is like to be scared. I promise you, you will be all right. It is my job to be sure you are okay."

They nodded.

"Now tell me what happened."

Chapter 10

The Forest

Spring 1941

Something inside me had changed and I knew it. I could feel it. I'd stopped crying.

It wasn't that I didn't feel sad anymore. I did. I still longed for my parents, and my family consumed nearly all my thoughts—daydreaming of what it was going to be like when I finally found them again, imagining when I would be able to jump into their arms, anticipating when we would all smile and hug and cry with joy. But I didn't cry about not being with them anymore.

I balanced on my elbows, squinting at the sun rising behind the trees. Spring had filtered its way into the grove and pushed the frozen winds of winter north, off into the distance. Now the air felt warm and dry. New leaves glittered off the blue sky, and the only sound was the breathing of the other kids nearby. My gray woolen coat—the one given to me at the start of winter—was damp with dew. Wiping it with my hands didn't work. I stood and shook it, spraying the drops in every direction.

I was hungry. Was there bread? Soup? Anything?

No one else was awake so I knew this was not the time to ask. Lying back down, I crumpled the coat underneath my head and used it as a pillow. I made shapes with my fingers, my thoughts drifting back over the last months.

There was the farmer and his wife and their barn where I had slept surrounded by hay and straw. They were kind people. They had fed me and given me blankets for the cold evenings. I had grown close with their sons Wladek and Wacek. Both boys spent many evenings with me, sometimes even sleeping in the barn though their warm beds, by the fire inside, were waiting for them. Wladek, in particular, had become my friend. Clothes he'd grown out of, I'd find folded in the stall where I slept; he taught me how to control the horse, use tools, and watch over the animals in the pastures behind their home. He also stayed with me when the Germans came, hiding with me in the pig sty, huddled under the trough, our hands over our mouths, holding our breath so we didn't move and creak the floor or shuffle the planks behind which we'd barricaded ourselves.

The Germans had come more and more frequently as the months passed. Sometimes they marched by, ignoring us. Other days they rode to the farm in trucks, stopping to collect taxes—money, food, and clothing—combing through the house, the barn, and the fields looking for anything they thought had value, and then driving away. Wacek and his mother and father always waited impassively, not helping them, not confronting them, not showing them that they were scared. Spitting at the ground as soon as they were gone, Wacek's father seemed like he might someday disembowel a soldier just because he was sick of it. He never did, despite my fears, and I often wondered whether he knew that if he did his family would be murdered and I would be doomed as well.

By the spring the Gestapo were coming nearly every day, not just to our farm but to all the farms nearby, traipsing about in their tall black boots, the bottoms of their coats becoming soiled as they kicked up mud, their faces growing more and more grim as they took inventory of what was there for them to confiscate.

One day in April, Wladek's mother took me aside. "It is too dangerous for you to stay here any longer."

I insisted it was the safest place I could be, but it was no use. "For you, and for us," she said.

"Mother, where can he go?" Wladek said. "We cannot just put him out. The Nazis will find him and kill him."

"They will find him and kill him here as well soon," she said. "And when they do, they will not stop with him."

No one spoke for several minutes, and in the silence I recalled the day a few months earlier when Wladek and I had taken the wagon, filled it with hay, and ridden back to Krasnik. I'd begged him to take me, to give me a chance to see my family, to let me hug my mother and father and Herzil and to bring them some of the bread and chicken I'd hidden under the seat. So much time had passed without a word, I had begun to feel as if I might disintegrate into sand if I did not speak to them, and tell them I was fine.

But they were no longer there when we'd arrived. The room in which we'd once slept was empty, and no one seemed to know them or remember that they had been there at all. "Check the trains," someone said. "God help them," another man mumbled, hurrying away. Wladek had looked at me, his face ashen with worry and concern.

Circling the neighborhood, then, I peered at every face and studied the coat and hat of each passerby, praying I'd catch just a glimpse of something familiar. I listened to the conversations of the people in the streets, hoping to hear a voice I knew or—if I didn't understand them—an accent to which I was accustomed. Nothing, however, was recognizable. There was no one left there that I knew.

That night, as we rolled back toward the farm in silence, cold surrounded us. Wladek seemed like he wanted to speak, to comfort me in some way, to offer a hopeful scenario where they were all safe in hiding or across some border in an imaginary refuge, living in peace, looking for me as well. He didn't say anything, as if he knew I would see through any convenient lie.

Finally, he cleared his throat.

"How long will you stay with us, Szmulek?" His question made my mind race; made my memories of the past months collapse into a murky swirl.

I didn't know what to say. It wasn't up to me, or to him, either, it turned out.

The next day, notwithstanding my insistence that he couldn't go, Wladek was hitching the horse to the wagon, filling burlap bags with my few items of clothing, and gathering a small satchel of bread and cheese, preparing for our journey. I remember him trying to convince his mother he could hide me, conceal me from the Gestapo patrols that came again and again. I remember waving to them as Wladek and I pulled away, and I remember Wladek, having dropped me in the forest, saying, a crack in his voice, that when the war was over he hoped I would return to their farm and stay with them again. "Go now," he said, his face filled with anguish. "Through those paths. There are other Jewish families hiding."

*　*　*

"Szmulek, are you awake?" My friend, Halez, was lying near me in the field where we had been living together amongst the other Jews with nowhere to go, enduring the unforgiving climate, for more than a year now.

"I'm awake," I said.

"Are you going back to see the Germans today?"

A few days earlier I had brought back a loaf of black bread and several raw beets from the German camp. The Nazi encampment was just a few miles from our forest enclave. Hundreds of soldiers there guarded tanks, trucks, howitzers, and cannons behind a barbed-wire fence. Eruptions of activity every morning were followed by afternoons and evenings of weapon cleaning, equipment repair, and planning for the following day: small groups of patrols gathering next to their vehicles, discussing whatever it was soldiers discussed.

Polish children, boys mostly, young and small, were let inside to shine the soldiers' black leather boots, wash out dirty shaving cups, and pound blankets free of dust and grime. The soldiers laughed and kicked at the children when they passed nearby, sending them sprawling in the dirt. Entertaining themselves with their aim, then, the soldiers threw garbage and muck, howling when they hit their marks.

I told Halez I might go again today. "If I ask my father, may I go with you if you go?" the boy asked.

"No," I whispered. I stared at the sky and thought about what the farmer had told me—if you speak only

Polish and do only what they say, and never retaliate no matter what they do to you, they will give you food.

"Purtzer," I said to the guard at the gate, presenting my cloth rag for inspection, hoping that he understood I wanted to offer myself out as a "cleaner." I knelt at his feet and buffed his boot, glancing at his rifle in case he decided to crash the butt on my head. *"Purtzer,"* I repeated.

He knocked me over with his heel and I sprawled across the gate, coming to rest against a post. Mumbling something in German, he made several soldiers nearby smirk, but then nodded that I could pass inside. My heart raced. I might be able to bargain for food.

Jumping to my feet, I crossed into the camp and walked the corridor between the barracks. I wasn't scared anymore. I knew what to do now. When I'd first come, I couldn't breathe from the fear; my clothes became damp with sweat; blood pounded against my temples. I'd been told that Polish children were tolerated, accepted as an annoyance, used for work no one else wanted to do; sometimes even treated nicely, sympathetically if they looked hungry. A Jewish child, I was warned, would not be looked at with similar generosity.

Now I'd done this a dozen times. My confidence was gaining. I knew the rules to follow.

Don't lead them back into the forest. Circle through the village nearby before entering, and leave the same way.

Do not speak. Work. Wait for food and then return,

hiding whatever you received under your clothing or in a burlap sack.

If you hear the word *Juden* spit at the ground.

Do not urinate inside the camp. Someone might see your circumcision.

If a soldier was cleaning his rifle, he would often be interested in clean boots as well. If he was shaving, fetching water was always appreciated. Writing a letter meant his helmet was probably off and needed rinsing. Bread or candy or a can of one kind of food or another was exchanged.

These were rote to me now and my nine-year-old legs stepped with poise through the groups of soldiers sitting on ammunition crates or on the steps to their sleeping quarters grousing at me as I passed. I understood nothing they said, but I ignored my lack of comprehension and thought only of the food I might soon be consuming.

A soldier motioned for me to approach. Sitting on the fender of a truck with five men, he swayed slightly and the others pushed at his shoulders. Shrugging them away, he turned to me, stuck out his leg, and pointed to his boot, barking at me in German. Did he have any rations or anything else I might want? His uniform was askew and disheveled. A long scar crossed over his nose and made a line down his cheek. His foreign commands became louder and more urgent.

Kneeling, I burnished the leather of his boot, starting at the shin and working my way down. The others pointed to spots I missed and laughed to one another. Without thinking I licked my hand and dampened the leather using my spit, then shined the wet spots.

Mimicking me, one of the soldiers spat at the ground before he rose and shoved my face into the outstretched boots I was cleaning and then into the dirt. Lifting myself, I went back to the job, shining the leather even more vigorously. Something felt wrong. This was not what usually happened. Usually I did these tasks, got rewarded, and left. Usually, there were three or four of us kids, who looked out for one another and distracted the soldiers if events went amiss. Usually I was not scared. Now I was scared and I wasn't sure why. Don't speak, I counseled myself silently. A word in Yiddish now and they might just shoot me on the spot. Don't ask for anything. Just finish and go.

Pulling at my scalp, the scarred soldier leaned toward me, lifted my head, and stared at my face. I struggled to return to my work but his grip on my hair was too tight.

"Juden?" he said. His eyes narrowed. Several more sentences followed but *Juden* was all I could discern.

I tried to spit at the ground, but my head was immobilized, pushed up and forward while he examined my features. Saliva went everywhere, dribbling down my chin before dripping to the ground.

"Juden," he repeated, speaking now to the men around him.

Everyone responded at once, and though their words

were without meaning to me, I tried to listen to their inflections to determine the threat.

"W imię Ojca i Syna, i Ducha Świętego," I insisted, grimacing. I performed the sign of the cross, though with my head in his grip it was difficult to move even my arm.

Releasing his grip on my hair, the scarred soldier pushed my face again into the dirt. I rolled onto my back and supported myself on my elbows and forearms, staring from one soldier to another terrified, praying in silence they would let me go.

Gesturing for the others to quiet, my tormentor pointed at me and began to yell. His face filled up with hate, his eyes burned with anger, and even though his words were nothing more than noise, I knew what doom sounded like. The others took turns, too, screeching phrases at me, some standing and glaring, a few growling from where they sat.

"No *Juden,*" I said. "No."

A boy I'd seen a day or two earlier walked by, stared at me, and then darted away. Three soldiers in perfect uniforms passed and glanced my way as well, but continued walking and talking, ignoring the situation as if it were happening a hundred miles away.

"So, you are not a Jew?" A new soldier had emerged from behind the vehicle. He was tall and his face was softer; free of the frowns of the others; his hair gray under the brim of his hat; scarless skin; eyes clear and blue and friendly. Was that a smile? A tiny turn-up of his lips into an affable expression? Was he here to help me? Please help me, I wanted to say.

"I am not a Jew," I said. "I am not..."

I stopped speaking and felt a hush spread like a cold wind across the scene. I'd understood this soldier and responded in the words I knew. I'd answered him in the language I was told never to utter.

"Your Yiddish is quite good," he said, speaking the Jewish dialect fluently.

With nothing more than a single nearly indistinguishable nod from him, the other soldiers descended upon me. The first blow was a kick to my stomach that deflated my lungs and sent a sword of pain up and through my shoulders. A second kick was aimed at my side, but as I winced and curled in agony, the swinging boot crashed against my temple. My sight went black and my ears rang and when I finally rolled over holding my head, blood poured down my fingers and dripped into my mouth.

They were tearing away my pants now, ripping them off my legs even as I reached for the waistcloth trying to keep myself covered. A fist hurtling against my nose made my hands rise to my face and I cried and made gurgling noises as my tongue became awash with warm red liquid. I could not fight them but I flailed anyway. Two men held me down.

"You are circumcised as well," the officer said without emotion, brushing off his sleeves as he spoke. "I will spare your wretched life if you do not lie to me. Now are you a Jew? Yes?" He grinned. "I already know the answer. So you may as well save me the trouble of having to order these men to beat you further."

Spit? Lie? Beg? The lessons I'd learned in the forest swirled in my head, but so did piercing pain. I stopped struggling. Every moment of my nine years seemed to flood into my brain. The cozy apartment on Kammiena #3. The yard. My family. Sleeping outside with Herzil. I was a Jew. I suddenly didn't care if they knew.

When Szmulek grows up, he will do things to make your life better. I am his good friend and I already know this is true. I heard Pinia's words echoing in my head and for a moment, defiance came over me.

"*Juden,*" I said. I spit blood on one of them on purpose. "Yes, I am a Jew."

That is all I remember.

Chapter 11

Memory and Escape

Columbia Point
1963

As I stitched myself into the Columbia Point community, I began to realize how much of my job amounted to simply being kind. I couldn't solve every problem the disadvantaged families in this neighborhood faced, but I could help out in every little way I knew how and that's exactly what I did.

I became a fix-it man and a marriage counselor, a nurse and a taxi driver. I helped with homework and chores, cleaned up graffiti, installed fences, and found lost dogs. I intervened in fights between brothers, and friends, and competing gang members, steered drunks to coffee, and guided people so stoned they couldn't distinguish which apartment was their own.

The kids of course were my main focus. Some of them had become so used to adults ignoring them that I noticed just being on the corner before school or in sight of the playgrounds in the afternoons would improve their behavior and give them a sense that someone cared. They teased me mercilessly about my accent and my clothes, cursed and sneered at me when I broke up a scuffle. And they tried to ignore me when I gave them advice. But none of that mattered to me—I could tell I was getting through. Even the ones who mocked me would sometimes come to me with their problems, looking for advice, and I could see they were pleased to have somewhere to go when something went wrong. It was a simple thing that anyone who endured a childhood like mine desperately yearned for.

I wanted to capitalize on this progress.

"Fifty dollars? For *this* bus? The seats are all torn and it looks like it might fall apart as soon as I pull onto the street."

He wiped his greasy hands on his already filthy sleeves and shrugged. "So you don't want it?" He turned to walk back toward his tiny cluttered office.

"This is for children," I said. "Poor children."

"Are you paying for it or are they?" he asked. "You look like you have money."

Exasperated, I took the last of the bills out of my wallet and handed them over. "Is it at least filled with gas?"

He shrugged as if he didn't know then disappeared around a corner.

Pulling myself up, I got behind the wheel.

I found a crowd of students gathered on the corner where I'd told them to meet me. "Okay, let's go," I said.

"Where are we going?" someone shouted.

"Cape Cod," another answered. "Don't you remember? To the beach."

They started to file in and I could see that the line stretched out well behind the bus and around a fire hydrant near one of the school buildings. Some were already in bathing suits; others had ragged towels.

"Did you bring the fifty cents?" I asked as kids stepped up.

No one answered but they kept climbing aboard.

"Fifty cents? Remember, I asked you to ask your parents for fifty cents?"

"Mr. Ross, I don't have fifty cents," Sam Killeen said. He was perhaps eight and had a full head of curly red hair that flopped over to cover his right ear. His expression was clear. He thought I was going to make him get out of line and go home. "My parents said they didn't have any fifty cents to give so if you really need it, they said, you can't go. That's what they said." He pleaded with his eyes.

I sighed. "Do you know a song?" I said.

"Sure," he said. "I know 'Danny Boy.'"

"Okay, good. You can teach everyone your song instead of paying."

He raised his eyebrows. "Really?"

I nodded.

"I know a song, too, Mr. Ross," a girl behind Sam said. "And my parents didn't give me any money, either. They said I didn't need to go swimming on any beach, no matter where it is."

"I know 'Yankee Doodle Dandy,'" someone shouted from down the line.

Kids were piling in now without even giving me their excuse for not having funds. Some simply shouted out the song they knew as they found their seats.

There was just enough room for everyone who showed up. I looked in my palm. I had seventy-five cents, but somehow I had never felt more rich.

"Okay, let's go," I said, squeezing in behind the wheel.

How I didn't lose anyone and how we all escaped without an injury, to this day I don't know. All I know is I tried to show the kids the best time they'd had in their lives and keep an eye on each of them the whole time. What I saw as they played together that day was that despite their hardships, despite the problems at home, despite some of their difficult prospects, they truly seemed to care for one another. The older kids helped me watch the younger ones and they shared towels and waded out into the water slowly with the kids who were afraid of the waves.

On the ride down and on the ride back, they took turns teaching each other their songs, and when someone forgot the words they just made them up and kept going. These were kids whose daily lives were filled with tensions now at their very happiest. Some, I knew, were living on the edge of catastrophe all the time. More than one had scars or bruises inflicted on them by forces that I knew were devastating and confusing at the same time. Others had afflictions that would probably last forever. Though they weren't survivors of concentration camps, their plights would likely leave some of the same lasting marks on them that mine had.

On this day, however, they would have the reprieve we all deserve.

Later that night when I finally lay down, it occurred to me that I hadn't thought about Dachau or Auschwitz or Krasnik or Feix at all that day. Had there been another day since I'd come to America when those memories hadn't made my heart race or my fists tighten? I couldn't recall one. I was trying to save these kids from suffering through their childhoods as I had, but they were saving me.

I had fifty fewer dollars than I'd had the day before, and I would have paid any amount of money for that feeling again.

I closed my eyes and hummed "Danny Boy" until I fell asleep.

Chapter 12

Dreaming of Home

Budzyn
Autumn 1942

The flesh covering my face did not seem like part of me.
It was swollen around my eyes and on the side of my jaw.
Features once pliable now felt like shoe leather. Where my
skin wasn't bulging, it was caked with blood: dried, stiff,
and scabbing mostly. Near my lips and cheeks the blood
mixed with the spit from my gaping mouth, oozing down
my chin and neck. Some parts of my face felt like weapons being used against me. Touching my nose, my eyes,
even my tongue sent bullets of pain shooting through me.
I realized there was no relief lying still and silent, so I
hoped I would die or at least fall asleep.

That did not help.

Breathing made my ribs ache. Straightening a leg or my back made it seem as if my bones were made of shattered glass cutting all my muscles. Blinking made flashes of nonexistent light magnify and sear my skull, and swallowing felt as if a fire had erupted and charred my throat.

I was alone. Before I lost consciousness I also realized I was naked.

Though my forehead pounded and my eyes would only partially open, I forced myself to examine where I was. Whatever I was lying on was stiff, coarse. Light was scarce, though there did seem to be a dull glow above me, shining in through a window.

In agony, I rolled onto my side. The room was big, broad, and nearly empty, like the barn I'd slept in outside Krasnik but without the hay covering the floors. Here the floors were barren, and the walls were lined with row after row of shelving, wooden planks supported by wooden columns, hastily thrown together, three levels to a row, barely four feet between each tier. I turned to look above me and found myself staring at a shelf, just a few feet from my face. I glanced to my right and realized each level was perhaps the width of a wagon, then a thin corridor, then another shelf. This continued the entire length of the building, shelf after shelf, nothing in between, nothing to alter the grim arrangement.

Was this a prison? Had the German soldiers beaten

me nearly to death and dumped me in some abandoned warehouse?

My parched throat gave me a feeling of utter desperation. Was there water anywhere? Even if it was here somewhere, would I be able to lift myself to drink?

I tried to move, to lift my leg and inch it over the edge of the shelf. My bladder was full, aching, so sore I worried it might be full of blood.

I relaxed and urine seeped out of me and onto my legs, warm and acrid. A pool formed, expanding, spreading over the shelf, dripping through the planks and tapping against the floor. For a moment the heat felt welcome, soothing, comforting; then the liquid cooled and my skin felt sore. I shivered. I thought about my mother, who would have been upset with me for peeing myself. She'll be mad, I told myself, when I get home and find her again.

The thought was a comfort.

"Please, another day I cannot do," I heard someone say. The voice was above me and was pleading. So many other sounds seemed to be drowning out the man speaking. An argument raged to my left, though I couldn't really make out the subject. Moaning and crying spilled from all around me. Snoring, gasping filled the air. "Please, no one should be kept like this," another prisoner announced to no one. "This is monstrous. Just kill us."

My cheek was cold and I realized I was lying on the

floor. Opening one eye and blinking, something told me it was night, but I wondered where I was. My face still hurt and I could feel stiffness throughout the rest of my limbs and back, but for a moment I had no memory; no idea of what was happening or why.

"Go to sleep, Graven," someone said loudly. "You're not helping."

I was in the barn with the shelves. But now it was not empty but full of men, all making sounds—of agony, misery, and apprehension. Looking up, I could see arms and legs, elbows and knees, feet and ankles all draped over the edges of the shelves above me. They seemed tangled, as if people were piled on top of each other.

Some had their eyes open, others closed. Some seemed to be staring at me, pleading with me, begging. Others looked right through me, as if gazing at something behind me, lost and hopeless. All of them wore the same clothing, gray woolen shirts and pants, most of them too big, with blue stripes. Some had head coverings of the same cloth. Some were scarred and bruised.

I looked down and saw that I also had on the woolen pants and gray shirt. My clothes were huge on my emaciated frame; they draped over my arms and legs, covering my hands and feet. Had someone dressed me and then put me on the floor?

I tried to reconstruct my memory of how I got here. I remembered that I had been beaten by the soldiers, but there was a gap between then and now. I wasn't as sore as I had been when I'd last woken up alone in this same room, but I was more frightened now amid all these strangers, these smells and sounds. Did they speak the language I spoke? I could catch some familiar words as well as languages I'd never heard. Even though I was surrounded by hundreds in the same desperate position I was, I felt utterly alone.

"Pinia says he knows you," someone said just loud enough for me to hear. "He said you used to play together in Lodz. Says you're the philosopher king."

I found the voice, two shelves above the floor. A face peered down at me, head and shoulders leaning out over the edge.

"Pinia is here?" I said.

"There are a lot of people from Lodz here. They brought all the Jews to work here. Some Polish Christians, too, if they didn't like them."

"Where are we?" I asked.

"Budzyn."

I squinted, confused.

"They make planes here, in the factory down the road. This barrack is where they make us stay. We're in prison, but they make us work."

"Where did I get these clothes?"

I could make out the outline of a man above me who was speaking to me. "Somebody died yesterday, so they gave you his." It looked like he was shrugging.

Hearing this, I wanted to rip them off.

"He wasn't sick or anything. He got hurt in the factory. Usually someone steals the clothes and wears two pair, but this time somebody took the clothes and put them on you. You're lucky."

I tried to chuckle and I coughed. The irony of the statement seemed lost on this prisoner, as if his life no longer had space for it.

We stared at each other, and as I started to make out his features I saw that the man helping me was a mere boy close to my own age. He reached his hand down toward me, and I shook it slowly. It was a gesture at once confident and sad, one that communicated so much to me: that we were not where we were supposed to be, that we were locked in some adult conflict that we might never understand. That we were probably going to die, and if we did it was by design. That there was nothing we could do about it.

But there was more. The boy smiled, and his face was filled with kindness, an indelible optimism. Nothing would darken his gentle core; no words or bullets, no sickness, no pain, no level of exhaustion could abate the humanity pulsing within him.

"I'm scared, too," he said. "I'm always scared."

"Is there any food here?" I asked.

"Not very much. A little piece of bread and some broth. That's all. Once a day. You missed it already."

A child began to cry, followed by a crescendo of voices asking for quiet, some buffeted by anger.

"Did you say Pinia was here?"

"Yes."

I searched the room around me, trying to ignore the stinging in my eyes.

"He sleeps across the yard. In another barrack, with his father. He said he knows your whole family."

"Is my family here?"

"I don't know." There was a shrug. "Most of us don't know anyone here."

There was a sharpness in his eyes now that told me I'd reopened a wound. I squinted to make out his face, thin but round, cheeks full and smooth, shoulders slender and narrow, eyes wide and clear, and nose tiny and red, as if from a cold.

"How long have you been here?" I asked.

"I can't remember."

"Are your parents here?" I couldn't help but ask.

"No," he snapped. "The police brought me here."

"Do you work in the airplane factory?"

"Sometimes," he said.

I felt a teardrop. His features had creased into a grimace.

"How old are you?" I asked, trying to divert the conversation.

"I'm eleven. We need to sleep now. They will wake us up before the sunrise for roll call."

"Roll call?"

"They count us. They make sure we're all here. Sometimes they kill people." Sliding back over the shelf, my
new friend disappeared from view.

Questions filled my head as I curled up, resting my
head on one arm. Did that mean they were going to kill
me at roll call? Where were all the other kids from Lodz
he had mentioned? Would I ever get any food?

That night I dreamed of home.

How many days I had gone without water or food, I did
not know. What I was clear about was the actual pain
I felt from thirst and hunger. These miseries were like
twin parasites consuming my insides, spiraling up from
my lower abdomen, circling through my stomach and
winding their way in a crisscross past my lungs, into
my shoulders, and down my arms. The wretched trail
seemed to burn. I was surprised that it hurt so much,
unprepared for the overwhelming longing, shocked by the
raw strength of a feeling like thirst. A threshold had been
passed. It was no longer that I simply *wanted* liquid or
food; not having them was killing me.

"Don't move. Don't let them know you're hurt. Don't
speak." I was surrounded by four men as we stood in the
dirt yard outside our barrack. They were each dressed as
I was, and though their woolen gray rags fit them more

readily than they fit me, the clothes still hung off them like loose curtains. "If they see that you're weak, they will shoot you," one man whispered.

Between the men huddled around me I tried to examine my surroundings. The yard was large and crowded, overrun really, with groupings just like mine, clusters of five, in lines as far as I could see, thousands of people. Buildings, barracks identical to the one I'd I exited on command a few minutes earlier, stretched out in rows behind us. Surrounding the barbed-wire fences that served as the barrier to the grounds, trees encircled the compound; tall trees thick with leaves and dark needles. Above me gray skies hung low and were so similar in color to our mandated attire, I had a moment's fantasy that I could disappear into a cloud, use the drab overhang as camouflage, and drift off back to Lodz, back to my mother, back to our apartment.

"Kill me. Please, kill me," a man screamed to my left.

Peering over the hip of the man blocking my view, I searched for the voice. "Be still," a man beside me said. He rested a hand on my shoulder. "That one is already dead."

"Please, have mercy on me. Please." Naked, a man stood beyond the fence, his hands holding the razored wire at his chest, his body swaying, knees buckling. I noticed then that he was not outside the fence but between fences, the barbed wire running in two rows, perhaps three feet apart, maybe less, he, imprisoned between them. Blood dripped down his torso like globs of paint. He looked like my father after butchering all day.

He was an old man, his hair nearly gone except for a few wisps over his ears; his body devoid of muscle, his skin hanging loosely over his elbows and knees, his ribs perfectly outlined.

I looked away and tried to think of something other than the pain he was feeling. I gazed at the ground, at my thighs, my calves, my ankles, then lower, at my shoe-less feet. The long legs of my pants were folded beneath them. I'd walked to this spot using the cloth as soles. The others around me had shoes, or something akin to shoes anyway. Whether they had arrived with their tattered footwear, stolen it, or somehow received it through some horrible requisition process, I had no idea, but the total disrepair made me sure they were no better off than I was. Blackened toes protruded from the leather as did bloodied insteps, nails that had cracked or been torn off altogether.

Several soldiers standing between us and the fence began to shout at the man caged inside the barbed wire, pointing pistols at him, threatening him.

"What will happen to him?" I whispered.

"He died three days ago, when they put him in there," the man beside me muttered.

"Shh," came a scolding reply.

"Why are those men not in line?" I asked as quietly as

I could. Milling about near the screaming soldiers were ten men dressed as we were, but their attire seemed clean, fresh, and new. Red triangles of cloth were sewed into their shirts, and each wore a yellow armband with a Star of David printed in blue. Snug-fitting caps covered their heads, and all of them were shaven and hearty. Three had clubs, and two others had knives tucked into their belts.

"Capos," a man behind me said. He spat. "Worse than the Germans."

Slumping, the man pinned between the fences let his arm fall against the barbs of the wire. Blood sputtered but he rubbed his wrist even more vigorously against the sharp metal until his skin was open and gaping. A man who I assumed was one of the capos approached him and kicked the fence, sending him sprawling backward. His arm, still stuck on the wire, contorted, and flesh tore off from his hand to his elbow. The capo kicked again, then turned, flashing a look of disgust at me and the other observers.

Confusion made me gaze from one man to the next around me, looking for answers to the questions I did not ask. Who were these men, these capos? Why were they doing this? They spoke and looked like Jewish Poles. Then it struck me. This was how they got food and water. This was how they got warm clothing. This was how they avoided being tortured between the fences.

I wasn't angry. I was so hungry, so thirsty, so thoroughly

beaten that for a moment I wondered how I could get this job. I thought I might vomit but my empty stomach just seized up and took away my breath. I thought about their families. Would they kick their own children, beat their wives and mothers and fathers for food? Would I?—and if not today, what about next week, next year? How long would I be able to hold on to my humanity?

The shout of a pistol echoed, and the crowd was silent. I straightened. The man inside the fence was dead, a bullet having sliced through his eye, his mouth slack and filling with blood, his body crookedly hanging from the wire barrier. With smoke still drifting from the pistol barrel, a capo handed the weapon back to the soldier who'd apparently ordered him to end the man's life. The soldier dropped the gun into his holster and snapped it into place.

Dust clouds rose at the far corner of the barrier near what appeared to be the only gate to the compound. A vehicle approached. The men around me looked tense. Nearly imperceptibly they separated, moving inches farther from one another, as if they wanted somehow to stand alone, not be complicit with whatever it was that might get someone else killed. Their faces had displayed inevitability before the death of the man in the fence, but now they betrayed fear, worry, a sense of being lost. I didn't know what was happening, but I knew to be terrified.

Wheels locking, the vehicle skidded to a stop. From

the open top, a soldier jumped to the ground, though one of the capos had moved to help him with the door. "Feix," I heard someone whisper. Two other soldiers remained in the car, both studying ledgers of some sort, ignoring everything, looking up only to take papers from another soldier who dutifully handed them over before snapping to attention and raising his arm in the Nazi salute.

With a chilling calm, Feix examined the dead man at the fence. A minute passed and he did not move. My heart sputtered. Just yards away, I could see even through his calm that he was enraged. At who or at what, I did not know. Was there something more than this man's death that Feix wanted? Could he be mad that the soldiers hadn't just left him to bleed out and rot alive on the fence? Feix didn't look like a monster. He looked like every soldier looked to me—sturdy, hair tightly combed beneath his cap, clean-shaven, black boots up to the knee. A straight nose complemented his face. A dimple creased in his chin. There was nothing out of place, no scar across his cheek or mark on his forehead that might have meant he'd been abused or beaten and felt a need to lash out. He wasn't fat or thin or ugly or sickly looking, wasn't burned or crooked or stooped or grotesque. The most horrifying thing I saw that day was how plain this soldier was.

I couldn't stop myself from being haunted by a question: What invisible forces exist in the world that rot a man so thoroughly?

Turning, Feix drew a pistol from his belt and without hesitation shot three prisoners in the head, one after another. Each of them crumpled to the earth. A child was left standing, staring at Feix, paralyzed. He was a boy not much younger than I was, with the same oversize clothing, the same frightened eyes, the same prayer clearly swirling in his head that his mother, his father, some good soul might save him. Feix fired again and the boy's corpse fell on top of the others.

"Please help me," I whispered, a prayer, my breath shallow, skin cold with sweat. "Papa, please help me."

But I knew no one could, not here.

Prisoners began to trudge away. I stood, watching Feix climb back into his car and signal the driver to pull away.

Chapter 13

The Man Who Lost His Way

Vermont
June 13, 1959

The long drive to Goddard College always seemed to put my mind at ease. There was something about the rural roads, the tree-filled scenery, the leaves turning, that allowed a sense of peace to fill my heart and keep the cruel memories at bay. Passing through I would see the tiny shops, the moms inside them holding their children's hands, the signs for fresh maple syrup and country inns. At the junction I always noticed the families gathered and campers waiting near their fires. The love they showed each other soothed my soul.

"Where are you headed?" I leaned toward the passenger

window and called to the man whose thumb had been out as I passed. I had slowed and finally stopped. I knew that the dangers of hitchhiking were real, but at the same time I cared about people down on their luck—I knew how little it took to get there.

"North," he replied, motioning with his head.

His mannerisms were odd. Instead of thanking me, he sat silently, fidgeting nervously and constantly patting his coat pockets as if checking to be sure he'd left nothing behind. Sweat, I noticed, beaded on his temple despite the cool temperature.

"Perhaps you're headed home?" I suggested.

"Perhaps it's none of your business," he said.

"I did pick you up when I didn't have to, so I was just hoping for a little conversation."

The tapping became faster.

"A little conversation," he repeated. "Okay. How about you pull over right there and then give me your wallet." His hand disappeared into his coat and when it reemerged he was holding a pistol. Pointing it at my torso, below window level. I could see that he was trembling.

I pulled over onto the shoulder. Fields spread out before me on both sides of the car. Glancing at the mirror, I could see that the road was deserted and that rescue was not coming.

"You're not much of a criminal," I said, relaxing into my seat.

"I have the gun, so maybe I am," he said.

"I've seen criminals," I said. "You're not one of them."

"Are you a cop?"

"No, I am not a policeman."

"So when did you see criminals?"

When I rolled up my sleeve, my number came into view.

"What is that?" he asked.

"You know what that is. Do you honestly think I am afraid of you or your gun? Do you have any idea what I have seen?"

He didn't respond.

"I know how men look when they are ready to kill other people. I have seen the faces of that kind of evil."

We both pulled ourselves out of the car. When he closed the door, he sucked in air and his shoulders slumped. He lowered the gun.

I tried my best to comfort him, saying I wanted to help. We stood there beside the road for a few minutes not saying much. He was kicking at the ground, as if he was digging for something in the asphalt.

"Why did you pick me up?" he asked as if it were my fault that he was trying to rob me.

I ignored him. "I saw men just like you, your age, shoot children down in cold blood. Hundreds of children lined up waiting for food. My friend Pinia. So many others I'd talked to just that morning." I shut my eyes to make the memory go away. Afterward they piled up the bodies and burned them. "That is what I have seen."

"Why did you pick me up?" he said again, anguish filling his voice.

"Why do you want to point a gun at me?" I replied. "Let's get back in the car."

The man followed me in. I was determined to find him some sort of help.

"I'm hungry. I just need some money."

"You could just ask me for money," I said.

"Why would you just give me money?" he asked.

"Why wouldn't I?" I said. "Why would I want you to go hungry? I know hunger. I don't want anyone to suffer such a thing."

"Take this," he said. He pushed the pistol toward me. "I don't want it."

I studied the gun in his shaking hand. It was no longer pointed at me, and I could see how its handle glistened with sweat. "Let's throw it in the next river we pass."

He nodded and reached for the door.

"Where are you going?" I asked.

"I am going to leave you alone," he said.

"Not until we find a place for a sandwich," I said. I pulled back into the road. "I'm hungry, and I need your help finding the best damn sandwich in this town."

Chapter 14

Work and Death

Over the next days I learned more of Budzyn. Each morning we lined up to be counted and stood in the open yard praying Feix would not appear, hoping no one near us might collapse and draw attention, grateful that no one had suffered enough that they'd decided to kill themselves by defiance. The sun had just begun to push darkness over the horizon when roll call commenced, and every morning the capos, taunting us, would hover around, all holding mugs of steaming liquid, sipping, appalled that the contents were still too hot, then sighing once the temperature had cooled to their liking. I took to imagining the mixture swirling in the cups, pretending I was washing sugary cocoa or honey-drenched tea over my tongue, letting it drip down the back of my throat, tingling my insides with sweetness. Sometimes tears overwhelmed me when I daydreamed of these pleasures. Engaging in evil, I began to believe, was the only path to sharing in such good fortune. I worried I would stoop to the level of the capos if I could—that my environment would force me to—and I cried.

What we were actually given to eat was incalculably little. Bread, both moldy and stale, came in half slices and was provided to us once each evening, together with a filthy tin bowl of salty, flavorless broth. Dispensed from a makeshift table cobbled together from sawhorses and boards, its meagerness dissuaded no one. Overwhelmed by urgency, we ignored any sense of decorum, order, or peace. And it was this dissolution of our mutual humanity—a direct aim of the Nazis—that was utterly horrible. We were made to be so desperate that we lost our camaraderie, forgot who and what we were. Queues dissolved into brawls, and even children were pushed to the back of the crowd. I joined in. Once I could move, I pushed myself into the line, punching at testicles, legs, knees, or whatever blocked me until my path was clear. Seizing my portion, I ran, using the bread to cover the broth so as not to spill a drop, anyone daring to chase me knowing they would lose their precious position in the disintegrating line.

Water, also, was dispensed once each day, spilling haphazardly from hoses controlled by the capos, who amused themselves with deceitfulness and the capacity for being unkind. Every inmate, holding a container of one kind or another—a bowl, a bottle, an old canteen, or sometimes even a hat or an old handbag—ran toward the spray, their arms outstretched, hoping not just to fill their pots but to feel water on their skin as well. "That is your ration, splashed on your face," the men said to several begging prisoners before turning the hose elsewhere. "Come back tomorrow if you'd like to drink." Over and over this deception occurred. If these men only knew the level of abhorrence rising in the barracks, I thought, if only they knew that if the opportunity ever arose nearly every inmate there would tear them to shreds.

The latrine, at the far end of each row of barracks, was the most foul place imaginable. Dysentery ran rampant. An overflowing pool of shit and piss filled the trough, baking in the overheated space, the stench making most people vomit as soon as they entered. Flies and other insects swarmed. Maggots piled in the corners, and roaches in armies ran along the floors and over the thin wooden platform that served as a pedestal from which to expel whatever waste came from your bowels. My eyes watered and bile rose in my throat every time I hobbled inside. When I was able to go, I wiped myself with newspaper, a shred of rag, or my hand, whatever was most available at the time of need.

I also learned that every morning, just after the count, an exodus occurred, the men gathering themselves again in the yard before marching through the gate in four single-file lines, heading to the factory down the road where some airplane part or gun was being manufactured. What they actually did or how they did it was not information anyone deemed me worthy of knowing, but I did wonder as I watched them trudge off each day whether building weapons was tantamount to committing suicide. If these war machines helped the Germans prevail, we would be locked up in Budzyn forever, providing free labor until they starved us to death or we met some other horrible fate. If only there were a way to refuse to help them, I thought. But I was old enough to see that death was waiting either way. Refusing to manufacture meant being shot, and working meant aiding the enemy and being murdered as soon as your strength disappeared.

The boys at Budzyn, at least those who were near my age, did not go to the factory. Most worked in the kitchens, preparing food for the German soldiers, peeling potatoes, cleaning carrots and onions, washing bowls and utensils. Younger children had jobs as well, sweeping out the guardhouses, raking the grounds, cleaning boots and buttons, and occasionally milling outside the fence, trimming weeds and grass that had overrun the barriers. Uniformed women hovered over these slave-children, scolding them to complete tasks more efficiently and completely. How these women came to these jobs and to the callousness they displayed was as odd and bewildering as anything I saw in the camps.

Chapter 15

Intervention

South Boston
February 6, 1962

Whitey's bar smelled of urine and vomit. It reminded me of the barracks at Budzyn. I hesitated at the doorway as if my body wouldn't obey my mind's instructions to enter. At a booth against one wall a man lay hunched over a table, a trail of spit running from his mouth to his outstretched arm. In another corner a woman, sitting on the floor, smoked a cigarette with a shaky hand. The bartender nodded. It was ten thirty in the morning.

"What'll you have," he said. His shirt was stained, his face unshaven.

"The sign out front says that you don't open until noon," I said.

"What are you, a cop?" he asked.

"No, I don't care when you open actually," I said. I looked around. "Although perhaps a little later might be helpful to some of these poor people."

"Maybe you should just go," he said.

Several patrons seemed to take notice of this request.

"Not quite yet," I said. "I am looking for someone."

"And who might that be?" he asked.

"I am looking for someone named Henry," I said loudly, peering around the bar. "Tilly's father. Are you here?"

My volume seemed to make everyone stir. A rustling and repositioning of chairs and stools followed.

"Henry, Tilly told me you'd be here. She says you're always here."

"I told the little brat to keep her mouth shut," a man muttered from the other side of the bar. "What do you want? You're disturbing everyone."

All eyes were on me as I made my way around the stools and chaotically placed tables and chairs.

"Your daughter hasn't eaten today. She went to school hungry. She went home and had nothing last night for dinner, either."

"I've been busy. I'm looking for a job."

"It's not even eleven in the morning and you're at a bar. Unless you're applying to be a bartender or for a job cleaning up other people's used bottles, I'm not sure I think you're making much of an effort."

"What do you care," he said.

"That's a good question." I pulled a chair beside him and sat. "Here's the thing. I have to see her every day, and I can't stand to see her as hungry as I was as a child. Her pain feels to me like—"

"She knows how to take care of herself," he said.

"I was at your apartment an hour ago. There are roaches everywhere, filthy dishes on every counter, the laundry has piled up in a corner, and there is no food. I fed her breakfast when she arrived at school. I've been doing it for a year. She finally told me where I could find you."

"So, good. She ate."

The bartender came over, shaking his head. "Henry," he said solemnly. "I want you out of my bar."

"He will only find another," I said.

The bartender walked to the other side of the room and began drying glasses with a rag.

"Why don't you go home and you feed your own kids," Henry said.

"One of two things is going to happen," I said. "I am going to walk out of here and have Tilly put in an orphanage where she will be taken care of and then hope-fully find a family that wants her, or you can get up and do what you're supposed to do, and I will help you find a job. The choice is yours."

He laughed. "This guy's gonna find me a job," he said. "What a load of shit." He took a sip from his beer. I nodded my head.

He stared at the table for a long time, as if there were some sort of puzzle in the waterlogged laminate that he was nearly at the point of solving.

He looked up at me. "You can really find me a job?"

"I've already lined it up. The only question is, do you want it?"

Chapter 16

Self-Preservation

Budzyn
Date uncertain.

Healing slowly for the lack of nourishment and water, I
slept most of each day, returning to my spot on the floor
after roll calls, drifting back to dreams of my father's lap,
of his kisses. My imaginings had taken on a quality of
reality that made it striking and shocking to wake. One
moment I was in our apartment, my belly full of bread
or a pastry from Pinia's father's bakery downstairs, my
mother washing my face with a cloth warmed over the
stove, Babsa hugging me and telling me to be careful on
the stairs. The next I was in hell, cuts and bruises everywhere, my stomach empty and aching, my parents gone.

Why I was allowed not to work, to sleep off my injuries, to indulge in these disconnected fancies, I did not know. Whatever the reason, I did not care.

"You look like you're feeling better." The gentle round face of the boy who had told me about Pinia was staring at me. "Are you better?"

I wanted to answer, to say I was, to say something kind, but I hesitated. Anxiety washed over me, confusion, panic. Something was amiss. I felt at the same time that I should turn away but also that I ought to return the kindness. It'd be years before I understood how my moral confusion was a result of the experiment I was surviving. In the moment I felt as if good air was no longer fit to breathe.

Weeks turned into months and my body healed, though without food and water cuts seemed to reopen more easily and my joints continued to ache. I was fairly certain I was nine now, though I could never be sure. I'd tried to measure my age by the seasons passing but between my time on the farm, in the forest, and in Budzyn, I'd lost track of the date. Many of the other children had lost count of their age as well, some announcing they were still the age they were when they'd first lost their families and no longer had parents to help track the passage of time. I met adolescents with the first growth of beard throwing shadows on their chins who said they were six or seven; young men working full shifts in the factory

announcing they were nine. It was as if when the Holocaust started, time had stopped.

Having been assigned the job of raking the grounds
of leaves and debris, I spent most of my tedious existence
thinking about food. Hunger was violently painful and
unbearably depressing, and the sheer weight of the relentless urge to eat made me at once lethargic and jittery,
passive but edgy. Fueled by starvation, arguments erupted
with other boys in the detail about who did more work,
who was stronger, whose parents might still be alive,
whom Feix might shoot next. Of course, constant scolding for talking reigned over us, the capo guards growing
more and more harsh and unyielding. Beatings became
common, the capos using leather switches or horse whips
to raise welts on the backs of our legs or necks, and if
someone dared mention food—said they were hungry or
cried for something to eat—they were pummeled by at
least three men acting in concert until blood ran across
the concrete floor.

The days when the capos were present, however, were
preferable. When they weren't there, when they were off
doing some other assignment mandated by Feix, the yard
filled with black-shirted guards—a separate company of
soldiers—a detachment of murderers who enjoyed inflict-
ing torture, and who had long ago abandoned any community or mercy. Children were pummeled arbitrarily,
no infractions required. Men were shot or bayoneted as

sport. And there were no rules or regulations proscrib-ing their wickedness or impinging upon their exercise of whatever malicious whim they could imagine. Where they were from and why they were their own band, no one knew, but we did know to be scared, and particularly careful, on the days of their reign. Running across an open yard became an exercise fraught with risk, a moving target being too enticing for them to pass up. Resting on the stairs to one of the barracks was an invitation to be decapitated, since machetes had found their way into their arsenals. Speaking in the yard, even in a whisper, left you vulnerable to their most adored cruelty, the excision of your tongue. And even the Germans seemed frightened, choosing to keep clear on the days when these sadists roamed the yard, huddling inside away from the mayhem, praying, I guessed, that the evil didn't turn inward and gather around the very men who had set the horror loose upon us.

Protecting myself had become my only impulse. I could see that no one cared whether I lived or died, ate or starved, breathed or collapsed. And so I became single-minded and relentless. I listened to every sound. I watched every movement. I took great heed of the hairs on the back of my neck. Suspicious of all things, fearful and wary, I felt as if I was on constant alert. Where the guards were with guns, whom the weapons were trained on, which prisoner was about to burst into defiance, I knew. If someone was sick, I stayed away. If a child cried, I made myself scarce. Anything at all that altered the routine made me skeptical. Calculating my existence second by second, I grew sullen and grim. I kept a distance from everyone, wondering constantly what had happened to my family, my mother, my father, Babsa.

Some of my questions were about to be answered.

"Szmulek?"

Roll call had come and gone and I'd begun my daily walk to retrieve a rake. Hearing my name said aloud startled me. I didn't stop.

"Do you remember me?" The questions were trailing me, but I was nervous. No one had spoken to me for weeks. I finally turned.

"Pinia?" I said and nodded. "Pinia. Pinia!"

He was smaller than I remembered but he was so frail his appearance may have deceived me. He'd had full red cheeks, clear wide eyes, and a belly that stuck out from under his shirt. His hands and arms had been meaty, his chin nearly invisible against his neck, his nose flat and wide. Now he was barely recognizable. Grayish circles surrounded his sunken eye sockets, bones were outlined with sharp edges from under the skin on his face, much of his hair had fallen out. Looking at him, it was clear whatever energy he'd once possessed had atrophied and been replaced with exhaustion. "Pinia," I repeated. I was suddenly petrified that I too had lost all of my physical features; that if my parents found me now, I, too, might be a stranger to them.

"My father told me to find you. To see if you want to sleep in our barrack. They won't care if you do." He started to weep and folded in against me. "I am so happy to see you. I missed you so much. I think about you, about us, every day and at night. Sometimes I dream we're back in our yard. Playing."

I hugged him and my eyes filled up as well.

"I think you can help us," he said. "Maybe you can talk to these men and tell them to let us go back home. I know you can do it. I see you do it sometimes in my dreams. You're talking to them and telling them we are good and kind and then they let us walk out the gate."

"They won't listen to me," I said.

"Will you try? I think you can save us. Will you try, Szmulek? Please."

Without thinking I backed away. I wasn't going to let Pinia's fantasy cost me my life.

"Pinia...I can't...they don't listen—not to anyone. They shoot."

Suddenly wary, I studied the yard to see who was watching, to gauge whether I'd be subject to punishment or death for this association. My eyes went from guard tower to guard tower to determine whether I was in a gun sight; whether Pinia's head was about to be spattered against the ground; whether some implement of pain was being gathered for use against me. The yard was quiet.

In the distance I saw the capos pushing into their quarters, a precious tiny human cargo being again led ahead of them, the group trailed by six German soldiers. I'd seen this parade over and over, nearly every day, the victims of these sexual predators sometimes, assuredly, too young to understand even what they were being ordered to do. I wanted to be mad, I wanted to feel a need to lash out, but I couldn't. Weakness, hunger, exhaustion overwhelmed me. Ignoring everything, I searched for Feix's car, for the black-shirted regiment, for the usual dangers, finding nothing.

I turned back to Pinia.

"Do you have any food?" I asked.

"No," he replied. "I'm so hungry."

Vague memories of myself as someone who played and laughed, someone who was worthy of Pinia's hugs and kisses and admiration, flashed in my head. I wished I had never lost that person. I couldn't understand how Pinia could recognize me when there was so little left of what he knew.

I took a long breath.

"Your brother is here," Pinia said.

"My brother?" I said, unclear of his meaning.

"Papa sees him sometimes. He says he's an electrician. He has a job in the airplane factory."

"Yes, Herzil was an electrician," I replied. "But wait—Herzil is here?"

"The skilled laborers have their own quarters, on the other side," he said. "My father sees him. In the factory."

Confusion cascaded over me. My senses took in this information as if I were in a dream, as if, had I looked away, turned, or closed my eyes, the entire landscape might change, the person in front of me morph into someone else.

"Herzil is here in Budzyn?"

Pinia nodded.

"Are you sure?"

"My father says he knows him. He might be able to take you to him."

Was this some trick of starvation, a way in which malnourishment had curdled my brain?

"They're coming," Pinia warned before darting away.

Two soldiers had turned to stare at us. I continued toward my rake.

Deprivation in Budzyn grew worse almost daily. Trucks so overloaded with prisoners that they moved haltingly—their axles curving, their tires at wilting angles—lurched into the yard, buffeted as they braked, then discharged wave after wave of bewildered and despondent men, hungry, exhausted, and filthy. Their expressions were, by now, so familiar to me I was no longer moved to sadness upon their arrival. Instead the calculation of how this off-loading was going to further reduce the already meager food rations ticked off in my head. Bread, which only weeks ago came in slices—albeit once each day—had first been halved as more men arrived, then quartered, and now would certainly be reduced to a single bite. Broth, which went from a bowlful to a cup, was henceforth likely to be a mere swallow. Water dispensed would now dwindle to a splash. And as more prisoners arrived and were wedged into the barracks, sanitary conditions would also further deteriorate. Dysentery and typhus would pass from man to man, through the air or oozing across open cuts as body piled against body in the cold. Mosquitoes and flies harboring germs and viruses incubating in the latrine would infect everyone. The lack of soap and water would make the stench even more sickening and vile.

The dead also began to multiply, reek, and harvest their own horrors. Not a morning passed when corpses weren't dragged out of the barracks, their clothing removed, their limbs stiff, mouths gaping as if they'd died in mid-breath, their eyes open, black, and vacant. Piles of the dead—naked arms and legs splayed and tangled, bones visible under paper-thin skin—mounded in the center of the yard, grew to a height greater than my own, and stained my consciousness. Every day I still wish I could forget the leaden thud of lifeless skin and cracking bones being tossed onto the heap, leaving a dreamlike pounding echoing in my ears. Once set ablaze, burning bodies, melting flesh, and human ash drifting on air currents became an apparition I'd see even in the light of day. And even long after the fire was extinguished, the pile disintegrated, the remains blown to the wind, I could still feel the dust of the dead on my skin and taste the caustic flavor of infirmity and slaughter.

Sleeping became my only respite. Though the barracks were overcrowded, dank, and filled with misery, I was able to sometimes lose myself in unconsciousness and for a few moments become oblivious to the overwhelming suffering. Around me, men forced to sleep on their sides, for lack of room to lie flat, wept openly for hours, or moaned of physical agony or begged for God to save them. Screams pierced the nights; primordial shrieks cursing at a deity who would not come echoed everywhere. Where there was not howling from men who could not fathom what was happening to them, the sounds of disease filled the room: coughing, hacking, the sound of a boy's breath giving out. The sigh of relief that it wasn't my own.

Every morning, the daylight brought new concerns. Upon waking, I would immediately examine my body. My hands and fingers were blistered and raw, calluses unable to develop. My elbows and knees were cut and bleeding, chafed by the cement I called my bed or by some prisoner near me who suffered from seizure-like flailings. Worst of all my body was digesting itself, using my muscles for food, keeping my heart beating by using my entrails as sustenance. Bones protruded from under my diaphanous skin. The machinery of my ankles and wrists was plainly outlined. My face had sunken into itself, my eyes protruding, my cheekbones sharp-edged under my temples, my chin a triangle under my lips. Compounding the agony of my starvation, my teeth began to rot and throb.

Discouraging as my condition was, others' fates were far more dire. Children, mostly boys younger than I was, could not withstand the plague of suffering, the pain and grief and neglect twisting their existence into hellishness. Left to weep, sitting in the yard, or unable to move from the barracks, these orphaned infants pleaded with anyone and everyone who passed to help them, to give them something, anything to eat, to hug them, comfort them, make the pain somehow go away. The soldiers who passed seemed to grow exasperated and impatient.

These forlorn and abandoned children, however, were not alone in becoming vexing to our overseers and terrifying to us prisoners. *Muselmanner*—what we called the walking corpses—multiplied our sense of dread. Deaf to any plight beyond the inner torment they endured, these were dead souls among us whom terror and starvation had killed without stopping their hearts. We could see them, but they could not see us. They did not need food, and cared not at all if they were beaten or maimed or if someone beside them had their head exploded by a searing bullet. The drowned, some called them.

They frightened everyone. Was their indifference contagious? Could their nihilism make you better prey for the Germans? Wandering, seemingly lost in the yard, failing to heed the warnings of the guards, they were shot in droves. But even as they died they appeared unconcerned. No pain flashed across their faces. They simply fell upon themselves, relieved, it seemed, for their anguish to be finished at last.

I watched them carefully from a distance. No one walked near them, fearing they'd get gunned down in the crossfire. No one spoke to them or reasoned with them, or attempted to shake them from the lethargy. No one dared even think about them lest sympathy develop into something more.

But for extended and tortured moments, I wanted so much to be them. When the hunger was so intense that it felt like a stake was being driven through my guts; when I felt so tired I thought my bones might just fall out and clatter against the yard; when I was so sad and lonely for my parents, it seemed like I lived in darkness all the time, I wanted to be them. I wanted not to feel anything any longer. I wanted not to worry whether I'd be alive the next day. I wanted one peaceful moment. Sometimes, I wanted to be dead.

That Herzil was here—somewhere—was the thought that I used to keep myself alive.

Days turned into weeks while I waited for Pinia's

I was selected for this Nazi propaganda shot aimed to convince the International Red Cross that prisoners were treated well. Presumably I was picked because I didn't look as malnourished as some of my fellow prisoners, though the belt, which I was given for the photo shoot, betrays that my uniform had already become baggy. *Courtesy of Steve Ross*

Piles of murdered prisoners awaiting mass burial was an everyday sight in the concentration camps. The camp pictured is not identified, but the horrific pile of bodies is much like the one I was thrown into, alive but unconscious, by a guard in Dachau. *Courtesy of the Library of Congress, LC-USZ62-92118*

Living in an orphanage in Garmish, Germany, after being liberated from Dachau, I started to put my life back together. Aside from my brother, Herzil, my entire family was gone, and I was not a teenager who knew how to smile. *Courtesy of Steve Ross*

After moving to Boston in 1949, I lived in another orphanage, where my roommate Berger emphasized the importance of education. I decided I would not let anything stop me from going to college. Thanks to Berger, education became the focus of my life. *Courtesy of Steve Ross*

I (far left) made great friends attending Goddard College in Vermont. For the first time in my life, I felt comfortable. *Courtesy of Steve Ross*

After I earned a master's in Ps
chology and decided I wou
devote my life to helping di
advantaged children, Govern
Michael Dukakis of Massach
setts (far left) swore me in as
member of the Board of Psychol
gists. *Courtesy of the Massachuse*
Governor's office

For many years I was a fixture
at the Saint Patrick's Day Parade
in South Boston. I would play
accordion at the courthouse while
many of the students with whom
I worked and their families came
by to celebrate. I would often
bring my two children (Julie is on
the far left, Michael on the right)
and introduce them to other
children from the neighborhood.
Courtesy of Steve Ross

I worked with many teams ov
the years, trying to make su
teenagers had opportunities
work together and build tru
and confidence. Here I am wi
a basketball team from Columt
Point that I coached in the 196(
Courtesy of Steve Ross

I was honored and humbled to receive the Boston Celtics' "Heroes Among Us" award for contributions to the community, and never have I felt so short. The Celtics organization has become active in educating people about the Holocaust. *Courtesy of Steve Ross*

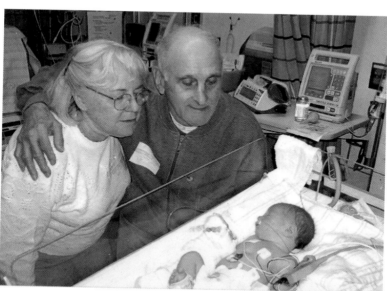

My life's partner, Mary, and me at the birth of my grandson Joseph. He was named for my father. Today, he is a strong eleven-year-old boy and an excellent hockey player. *Courtesy of Steve Ross*

With the support of then Boston mayor Ray Flynn, I rallied the local Jewish community to create the New England Holocaust Memorial. Here I am carrying a plaque on the day of the ribbon cutting in 1995. *Jay Fitzgerald/Boston Herald*

The opening of the New England Holocaust Memorial was a joyous event for so many survivors and their families. Ray Flynn (right) and I were relieved the day had finally come. *Jay Fitzgerald/Boston Herald*

I have returned to the memorial on many occasions. My son, Michael Ross (left), has helped me continue into my advanced age to speak about my experiences with an eye toward ensuring that the mistakes of the Holocaust are never repeated. *Courtesy of Steve Ross*

Watching white supremacists and neo-Nazis become increasingly active and emboldened in recent months has proved one of the most difficult experiences of my life, which has had no shortage of them. In the Summer of 2017, the New England Holocaust Memorial, which until then had never been vandalized in the twenty-three years since its construction, was desecrated on two separate occasions. The broken glass that lined it called to mind Kristallnacht, the pogrom in which Nazi forces ransacked Jewish homes, hospitals, and schools with sledgehammers, slaughtering 91 innocent Jews. *Boston Globe/Getty*

Despite the vandalisms, my faith in humanity to overcome hatred remains undaunted. Three days after the second attack on the New England Holocaust Memorial, 50,000 courageous Bostonians took to the streets, protesting a so-called "free-speech" gathering that had been organized by the Alt-Right to take place nearby, the recent murder of an anti–white supremacist demonstrator in Charlottesville, Virginia, and the desecration of our memorial. Only a handful of people attended the Alt-Right gathering. *Boston Globe/Getty*

father, Lev, to take me to Herzil. Anxious as I was to see him, I understood that it was both difficult to pass from one part of the camp to another without raising suspicions among the guards, and, more important, dangerous if anyone was caught in a place they were not supposed to be. Herzil, Lev told me, was in the skilled labor encampment on the far side of the compound, separated from us by more barbed wire and under the leering watch of the black-shirted guards we despised. Given the obstacles, I had to wait for the right opportunity, for Herzil to be free from constant surveillance many workers had to endure on the odd day when there were fewer guards.

"Your brother is pleased you are here," Lev told me, when he was able to pay me a visit.

This response worried me. Pleased that I was here? Why wasn't Herzil more adamant about finding me? Wasn't I important to him anymore? All I thought about was my family—all of them, Herzil, my mother, my father, all my brothers and sisters. It felt like they had they forgotten me.

Lev saw the concern on my face. "You must be patient, Szmulek. I promise. You will find each other soon."

Nodding despondently, I looked to him for more reassurance. Lev looked like a man who had at one time been robust but who after months or years in Budzyn had shrunk from malnutrition, leaving too much skin to cover what was left of his insides. He actually appeared weighted down by the empty folds of loose skin—even his forehead sagged over his eyes—and I thought he seemed to be the oldest man in the camp. Still, he was there with Pinia, and his son clung to him, ran to him whenever he'd return from his work detail, and they huddled and kissed and cried together. I loved watching them. I was so envious that they had one another. Their closeness and the seemingly endless distance between me and Herzil made me sadder than I'd even been before.

"Come up to our shelf tonight," Lev said, seeing that I was still downcast. "We will make room next to us, Pinia and I. You can come up off the floor for once. For sleeping."

I did, and I stayed with them, and as the time passed and still Herzil had not appeared, I began to fold myself among the eight others on the meager shelf, night after night, hoping to stay warm, hoping to drift off into dreams, hoping that the next day would finally be the day when my reunion might take place.

"Pinia, you have saved your bread."

"Yes, Papa," Pinia whispered, hoping, I was certain, that everyone else was sleeping. "I want to eat it in the morning before I have to sweep. I am so hungry in the mornings. I am hungry always but in the morning when I wake up I sometimes think I can't get up. I can't. I don't know what to do I am so hungry."

"Let me hide it for you, here in the folds of my blouse.

No one will find it there and in the morning I will make sure you have it before you have to work."

"You won't let anyone steal it, Papa, will you?"

"No, no one will steal your bread. You are smart to save it."

I lay next to them and wished my father was there. He would save my bread for me, too. I remembered him taking me to the seder, my school, and lingering after he dropped me off, telling me he would be there as soon as I was finished.

That night I had long and lovely dreams. Rosh Hashanah feasts were spread out on tables before me. Pastries with blackberry jam. Kapuszniak brimming with cabbage and meat. Eggs, boiled and roasted, potatoes sopped with butter, glasses of milk, and sweet dark chocolates. Running from table to table, filling my mouth as soon as it emptied, trying something new and then returning to what I'd eaten before, I gorged myself. And over and over the dream recurred, almost as if I could conjure it up at will.

Chapter 17

Pinia

As I trudged to the yard the next morning, my legs felt rubbery and flimsy. Cold had come during the night, infiltrating the ground, and clouds covered the sky, held aloft on brisk breezes. My feet ached as I passed from the barrack to the grounds. I winced while I walked, and my eyes began to water from the chilly air and the wind.

Something was wrong. More wrong than usual.

"Why did you eat my bread, Papa. I told you I needed the bread in the morning."

Pinia was in the arms of a capo, looking back at his

father in the lines, crying to him, despair and betrayal haunting his face.

"I'm sorry, my son," Lev called back to him, arms outstretched in a plea for forgiveness. "I'm so sorry. Please forgive me. I was so hungry. There it was in my clothing, then it was in my mouth. I didn't even know what I was doing, Pinia. Please forgive me."

"I'm so hungry," Pinia shouted back over the capo's shoulder.

"They are taking you for a meal now. They said so. Please forgive me. Please."

Drifting through the lines, capos were muttering instructions. I listened.

"If you are a boy working in the yard, line up at the fence with the others. The Germans have decided to feed you a nice meal. Outside the gates, in the forest, there are tables set up with enough food for all the boys here. Line up now if you work in the yard. Get in line along the fence. There will be bread and meat."

Lev's voice distracted me again. "Pinia, I am sorry. Please forgive me," he continued shouting to his son. "Now they will give you food. They know how hungry you are."

Queued up along the barbed-wire fence, boys fidgeted as more and more joined the line. Capos pulled some of the young away from the others and pushed them to the end. I stood and watched. Soiled and thin, tired and sick, drained and bruised: There was confusion and dread on all the boys' faces. Food had been promised, but not to the adults. Why had the boys been singled out? Because they were all so young?

Counting the boys in line, I felt one capo push me and another pull me in the direction of the gathering. "Go, go, go," they said in unison. "Get your food with the other boys."

Pinia was in line now, still sobbing, unable to understand how his father could have stolen from him. Feeling the crush of both Pinia's pain and his father's hunger, my thoughts spun in my head.

I continued counting and watching, sensing for the first time that something else was not right.

Outside the fence the black-shirted guards stared at the forming line. Inside, the capos worked harder than usual, their voices urgent, their movements oddly stilted, diffident, uncomfortable. I shivered.

"One hundred and six," I said quietly to myself as I stepped to the rear.

"We will go out to the forest, out to the tables," a German officer announced. "Then you can eat. All the boys will eat in the forest."

Sweat beaded on my forehead and my heart pounded hard against my chest. The promise of food was so enticing, so alluring, so overwhelming, it was all I could keep in my mind. But pinging at the back of my head was an alarm, a whispered warning, an impulse. I felt as if I was divided, half of me wanting to go to the forest and get the nourishment I so badly needed, that was promised, the other half commanding me to run. The world was insane, but could this possibly be some nefarious trick, I wondered, played only on children? The Germans were known to dispose of adults on whims, but lined up here were boys, all under fourteen. Twisting along the fence, the line seemed to be animated, bulging in spots, becoming concave in others. The guards tried to keep everyone still, facing front. But they seemed uneasy. Some looked like they were holding their breath or about to be ill. Running my eyes along the queue, I shuddered at how many we were, how filthy, how frail, how feeble. Would it be different after we ate? My eyes stopped on Pinia. Still whimpering, his head and shoulders sagging, his legs barely able to hold his weight, he had an expression of resignation I had not seen before in him. My eyes settled next on the capos. Whispering among themselves, their gazes were fixed upon the ground, their feet shuffling, their hands pulling their coats more tightly around them. Cries, then, from the captives still standing in the yard. Their faces were flush with pain, tortured faces, frightened faces, faces of such utter anguish I was thrown back against the boy behind me. But he didn't move. He didn't react. He saw the expressions also. His face was awash with terror. Capos turned to us. We'd made noise. We weren't going to get our food. But there was no food. Searching up and down the line now, the capos approached, but they weren't looking for us. Their eyes were up now, scanning. Some moved, walking to the gathering and pulling a child aside. Then others did the same, one child here, then another, pushing them into a circle near a German officer. Five, six, then seven. I knew them. I'd seen them before. There was Pinia's friend, who had spoken to me that first night in Budzyn; who'd cried when we next spoke; who'd tried to tell me something and whom I'd ignored with disdain. I could sense that the line was leading to our murder.

So I ran.

Darting left and circling two capos, I did not wait to see if they followed. Crossing into the men's line, I wove a crooked path, dodging around withered legs, bone-thin arms, and gaunt fingers all pointing at me as I passed. There was no outside sound, at least none that registered in my ears. All I could hear was my own breathing, air pumping in and out of my lungs, wheezing its way through my throat and out my nose and mouth in grunts. Was I running in circles? Dust was everywhere, choking me, blinding me. Was I about to be shot? Would I crash into a capo, a guard, another prisoner? The energy of terror pushed me, as if I'd been woken, electrified. My legs seemed to be only vaguely part of me. Were the black-shirted guards behind me? I turned and slashed, ducking past barracks and piles of the dead, and black boots, and guns, and weeping circles of pitiful prisoners and faces flashing up in feverish visions.

I found my way to the latrine, searching out anywhere to hide. Without turning back I contemplated my alternatives, and then lowered myself into the trough. The thick slime surrounded me, filling up my pants, rising above my waist, to my arms, to my neck. I gasped for fresh air and vomited.

Dizzy from lack of air, my senses folded upon themselves, my vision blurring, my hearing muffled. I thought of the boys wandering into the forest, prodded forward by guns.

I lay there for what felt like hours.

A heart-wrenching noise in the distance, piercing and hollow, broke me from my daze. The gunfire came in long blasts, strafing fire, a pause, then more, then more again. Sporadic bursts, a trench of soundlessness, then another orphaned bullet fusillade.

I couldn't breathe.

There hadn't been any food. Now 105 children were dead. Boys who'd worked in the yards. I prayed for Pinia and all the others.

Over the last months I'd grown inert, indifferent; I had begun to feel I didn't care if people died, if people starved, if people were tortured, if anyone was worse off than I was. Survival was all that was left, and worn down by the inequities, the cruelty and inhumanity, I'd lost my empathy, lost my sensitivity, lost myself.

But that was before I lost Pinia, my last connection to the happy childhood the Nazis took from me. For Pinia, I wailed. He'd asked me to help somehow, thinking I was so much more than I was. For him I'd somehow been a symbol of hope and peace and wisdom, one that had utterly failed him.

He must have wondered, as the bullets started to fly, why God wouldn't have allowed him that last piece of bread; wondered as his skin was being torn apart why his father, the man he trusted above all else, and his childhood friend could have betrayed him.

I wish I could tell you, Pinia, how sorry I am.

Chapter 18

Opening the Vault

Newton, Massachusetts
May 29, 1968

Something had overtaken me, my chemistry, my brain. My personality seemed hollowed out, as if someone had hacked it into pieces. I was struggling to rediscover who I was at the same time as I was struggling to just lead myself through the normal rhythms of a day.

For years after I left Dachau, in the orphanages, in college, and beyond, I showered obsessively. Standing under the water, letting it wash over me, scrubbing my skin often until it was raw, all part of a futile ritual that I repeated to try to wipe away the past. Living in filth, breathing in other people's shit, spattered with blood and vomit for years on end had played with my mind. Some-times hours would pass as I stood inert under the streams until all the hot water had drained. Soap was often not enough, either. I wanted brushes and occasionally even a scraper to purge my skin of the scars of my past. Early on, kids at school would stare at me, watch me make myself bleed from my compulsive scratching, running to get an administrator who would finally force me to the nurse for bandages and ointment. Even in my later years, after I was married and had children, I still sometimes found myself unable to escape the magnetism of the water. My five-year-old, Michael, cried when he once came upon me wide-eyed and paralyzed in our bathroom dripping, sim-ply not able to bring myself to leave. My daughter would run to her mother and ask her what was going on.

That was far from the only scar the camps had left on me. Besides my compulsive need to bathe away my past, I also couldn't escape the need to hoard everything and any-thing in case I needed it under desperate circumstances. A hubcap on the street was potentially a soup bowl, old newspapers could become toilet paper or be useful to build a fire if every other system failed, bottles and cans could be filled with fresh water to be hidden under the bed, old torn clothes were bandages or maybe even makeshift blankets. Food, too, was as precious as rare jewels. No scrap was left unwrapped for later consumption on my watch; no drop at the bottom of a milk carton was missed if it could be extracted; bones, vegetable cores, and seeds were swaddled and kept for another day.

"If only Papa had known what was coming, he would have used this or that," I told myself.

And there was one other compulsion I had for years after I was liberated: I was unable to talk about what had happened, as if I feared the truth would frighten people and I would find myself isolated once again.

These impulses still haunt me today—except for the last one, that is. My bedroom has books and newspapers stacked as high as my chest, as if to remind me of those we lost. These stains will be with me until I die.

Chapter 19

Herzil

As I blinked awake, confusion descended over me. Vague memories of running and filth, followed by retching and fevers, loomed at me like nightmares. Still, little resonated or made any sense. Where I was—this was a mystery. Beneath me, a straw sack mattress felt soft against my back; the room seemed warm and strangely clean, and the light of dusk filtered in from two large windows overlooking the bed. I also felt like I'd eaten—at least something—not that I wasn't hungry, but I didn't feel as if I was starving. I sat up startled. Was this some strange afterlife where children went to spend all eternity alone in an odd room?

I lay back and tried to remember.

It came back slowly, the hands, fingers stretching toward me. Words: "Come. Hurry, take our hands." Two men had rescued me from the foulness of the latrine, and I stood naked, shivering, being washed down with buckets of urine. "This is all we have for disinfectant. We must clean you. Be still."

I had dysentery so severe, blood oozed from my orifices. There were headaches and fevers when I'd find myself freezing one moment, tremoring with heat the next.

And then I remembered more.

Five men holding me down, one on each limb and another forcing open my jaw. A knife of pain at the back of my mouth. Searing visceral agony with a taste so acrid it tasted like nails covered in motor oil. A wire. My tongue being pinned against my cheek with someone's fingers, not my own. The wire again, this time being secured, wrapped around a tooth, clawing into my gums. A shocking explosion of torture, then blackness, warm liquid filling my mouth, tasting faintly like meat.

Then I woke up here.

"Herzil, his eyes. They're open."

I followed the voice. A capo standing at my feet stared down at me. Glaring back, I tried to recognize the face. His eyes were small and contorted into a squint. Wide at the bottom, his nose flattened against his cheeks and disappeared into his forehead. Whatever teeth he'd had were gone. Stubble covered his chin and cheeks. Outside, behind him, darkness had fallen.

"Herzil," he said again.

A man stood.

My memory of Herzil, over time, had capitulated to hunger and weariness. How long it had been since he bade me goodbye as I left for the farm, I had no idea, but somewhere across the months and years of degradation, he'd been transformed and given nearly immaculate qualities. No thought of him had come to me for as long as I could recall where he wasn't happy and animated: sitting with my parents, smiling; walking with me to the shul, grinning; improving the lights in the yard and enjoying the gratitude of the neighbors. In my mind he was hearty and talkative, witty and powerful, joyful and charming. In my brief memory he had been the smartest man in Lodz, the strongest soul in all of Poland, and the envy of all my friends.

The man before me was not that man.

A back, shrunken and stooped, shoulders wilting under their own weight, eyes that were vacant and lost, greeted me. He was more narrow in the chest than I remembered and concave nearly everywhere. Frail and pale, his face lacked animation, seemed to hang off his skull as if it were tied poorly from behind, drooped to his neck. He didn't appear sad, really; instead he seemed shy, embarrassed at his own circumstances, worn down beyond repair.

Jumping to him, I squeezed my arms around his waist, hugging him to me, smelling him, remembering him. I pressed my head into his abdomen and embraced him as if I could bring my entire family back if I just refused to let go. There was so much I wanted to ask, so much I needed to know, so much that I'd not allowed myself to think about for so long, I felt like I might burst. Still, for those few moments I just wanted to hold him, to feel like he might take care of me again, to believe I was loved by someone alive.

His arms hung at his sides.

I pulled back and glanced at the capo, a new fear rushing through me.

"Herzil, it's me, Szmulek. You remember me, right? Herzil?"

"He remembers," the capo said. "He's just inside himself now. Give him some time."

Panic nearly overwhelmed me. "A *Muselmann*?" I said.

"No. No, not that. He just pushes everything deep down to the bottom somewhere, and keeps his distance at the same time. He knows you. He's wanted to find you here for a long time. I tried to help but I didn't want to get shot, either."

My face apparently betrayed my lack of understanding.

"I'm Chapinski," he said, ignoring my confusion.

Staring at him, hoping for some guidance, I saw that he seemed to be studying his shoes.

"We all thought you were going to die," Chapinski confessed. "We had to pull out a tooth that was making it worse." He stood and put a hand on Herzil's shoulder. "Only God knows how you survived even one minute in that latrine. My mind cannot imagine such a thing."

"Where are we?" I said.

"Herzil promised to require your sister Anka to consider me in her long-term plans if I let you recuperate in my bed. So you're in my bed. I have always had a fancy for Anka. You could say something nice, too, when the time comes. It won't kill you."

No memory of the name Chapinski came to mind. His face was new to me as well.

"Are you from Lodz?" I asked.

"Nearby," he said. "I made milk deliveries. That is how I came to know your sister."

"Where is my sister? Do you know where any of my family went?"

"No one knows where anyone is. After the war, everyone will find their families."

"Does Herzil know where they are?" I turned to my brother and wondered if he could hear me.

"We all lost one another outside Krasnik. All the women were sent one way, the men another. The children somewhere different still."

"The guards killed all the boys that were here," I said, suddenly mad that Chapinski collaborated with the guards. "That's why I was in the shit. So they didn't kill me."

Chapinski went silent. Behind his eyes, behind his words about Anka, behind his friendship with my brother, lay something else. I could sense that the sound of the gunfire cutting down the children would reverberate in his head forever. He wasn't in the labor lines, he didn't sleep in the barracks stacked a dozen to a shelf, he didn't starve. And he stood by while these monsters did what they did while he accepted their offers to turn on his friends and the families he'd known for his entire life.

Averting his eyes, his face contorted in pain, then, after a moment, relaxed. Inhaling, he gathered himself. "As soon as you're well I will be taking back my bed," he said. "I will get you assigned to Herzil's barrack. That is all I can do. Any more special treatment and it would be bad for all of us."

"Will they kill me when they find out?" I asked with disdain.

"We'll make you into a spooler for your brother. Do you know what this is?" He spoke as if he wanted me to know he was doing me a favor.

I didn't answer. I lay and stared at the ceiling.

"You will unwrap the wire, make sure it doesn't tangle, and feed it to Herzil. From there he can make the planes. A good job. No one will kill you."

I turned away.

"You can thank me by telling Anka I was nice to you. Okay?"

I felt the bed shake and turned back. Herzil had lain down beside me.

"Okay?" he repeated. "Some nice words to Anka?"

Herzil pulled me close to him and started to cry. I could feel his tremors of sadness, but also the joy that he'd found me.

Like the rest of my family, the Herzil I knew was gone. What I'd hoped would be a reunion leading to an end of my misery—information about my mother, my father, my sisters; someone to care for me; relief from the hunger and deprivation—did nothing other than exacerbate my hellish existence. My brother barely spoke, and even when he did, it was clear that he was growing more sullen and increasingly bitter. I held fast to a fantasy about him, that he would be my defender, ensure that I was fed, guard me against threats and danger, but the truth was exactly the opposite. My eleven-year-old sensibilities, burned into my wary consciousness by years of mistreatment, seemed to be the only thing keeping us away from disaster.

Guards whom Herzil ignored—there were many—I distracted by making noise. When Chapinski complained, I feigned further illness and mentioned Anka over and over. If the other capos grew suspicious of Herzil in Chapinski's room, I ushered him outside, sat with him, and talked of Lodz until it was safe to return.

Herzil never thanked me; he didn't even acknowledge that I'd intervened. Still, I knew he wasn't gone completely, as sparks of compassion occasionally overwhelmed him. Tears sometimes came unannounced and without provocation. An intermittent smile warmed his face. There were even rare moments when he lashed out and seemed determined to sacrifice himself in the name of defiance. I loved those moments. They gave me hope and purpose. I nevertheless rarely let him out of my sight.

After I recovered, I began to work as a spooler in the factory where Messerschmitts were being fabricated. My job was to ensure that wire was dispensed in a uniform fashion, that there were no ruptures in the copper, and that no one was slowed by faulty materials. A spool around my waist, loaded down with more wire than I thought possible to tote, became my yoke. Weakened by my ordeal and lack of food, my knees frequently buckled, my shoulders sagged, and the guards eyed me suspiciously. Three days in I nearly gave up, deciding I would stop feeding the wire through entirely—until a familiar sound saved me.

"Herzil, what is that?" It sounded like my father's watch, beeping to announce the hour.

"Hush," he said.

"I know that sound." I was so overcome with nostalgia that I couldn't even begin to focus on my job.

"Be still. The guards will hear. You need to loosen more wire."

"Please, Herzil."

"Szmulek, do the job."

"Do you think I don't remember the sound of Papa's watch?"

Herzil pretended not to hear me. Focusing on an electrical panel, he ignored my exuberance. Pounding out wire, he drowned out the sound of the alarm; scraping sounds, metal on metal, wire rattling off fuselage, all served as cover. Finally, the alarm was gone.

"How did you keep the watch?" I asked.

He smacked me in the face. I turned to him in shock.

"Don't speak of it again," he said.

"Please, Herzil." I was breaking down.

He leaned toward me, his eyes narrowed and his chin became taut. "I am going to trade it for some bread. When the time is right. There is a man who wants it, a painter."

"But…"

"There are no buts. . . . We need the food. You need the food. Your legs, they are like matchsticks." He straightened. "Now unreel more wire."

I understood but something gnawed at me. This connection to my father, this heirloom, this symbol of our family, had been the only possession I could remember

across all of my time alive. The soothing soft monotonous
ticking, the pleasant ring, and the chain jingling off his
belt: These were the sounds of my happiness, the reso-
nance of the time before the nightmare; this was the measure of my memory of joy. I heard it and smells came back
to me—our kitchen, the bakery at the edge of the yard,
kapuszniak—my parents' touch, my grandmother's hugs,
children's voices filling the streets. The watch was not just
a timepiece, it was a museum of my life. But now we were
going to trade it for bread.

"May I hold it once beforehand?" I said.

"No," Herzil replied.

"But it was Papa's," I said.

"It is not available to be passed around now," he barked
at me in Yiddish.

"Just for a moment, Herzil."

"It is in my rear end, Szmulek. That is where I am hiding it from the guards. Do you want to see it now?" He
stood. "By the way, it is killing me. My ass is raw. If the
painter will come I will finally be rid of it. He promised
us five pounds of bread. One pound a day. I hope he's not
a huzzer."

The painter kept his word and once the watch had
been exchanged, for five days, behind machinery, hidden
from the guards, he passed my brother full round loaves
of beautiful brown bread. Nothing ever tasted so wonderful. My gums rotting, my teeth crumbling, my tongue

nearly numb: Still, tearing away pieces and letting them almost dissolve in my mouth brought me close to tears. Flavor. I'd almost forgotten what it was like. A sweetness, ever so slight in the crust, made my heart flutter and my mind flow back to treats I'd eaten at Purim, what seemed like centuries earlier. A salty texture to the meat of the loaf spread across each cheek and elicited a moistness—saliva—that I thought had long ago been lost. My eyes widened with each bite; my ears rang with a joy I'd forgotten existed; my skin tingled as I could practically feel the nourishment dispersing through me.

The first bites seemed to be gone before I'd even had a chance to realize they'd been consumed. I slowed then. Worrying that someone, anyone, might come and confiscate this bounty, I hugged the food close to my chest before savoring taste after taste, ripping off smaller and smaller portions in order to prolong the pleasure. Should I save some, keep it for later? Pinia came to mind; his father's inexplicable thievery. No, it is here now.

I had watched Herzil pass the watch to the painter and had felt a pang of loss, but for five days my belly was full. Strength bloomed in me and it was as if the sun were rising inside my body, reflecting outward, filling everything with warmth. A blur that had taken over my eyesight dissipated and finally disappeared. Sagging muscles woke. Bones ceased to ache and feel as if they were scraping together. Blood flowed and my purplish skin turned ruddy. Finger- and toenails that had turned to paste, hardened. Eyelashes stopped falling out in clumps. A song—one from the yard in Lodz—played over and over in my head.

The weight of the spool is gone, I thought. My legs are able to carry me.

"Herzil," I cried out, "I can stand."

"Are you trying to get us all shot? Give me wire and make sure your mouth stays shut."

Even his harsh words could not weaken my exuberance. Survival suddenly seemed possible. Visions of us once again in the yard in Lodz consumed my imagination. War would end, and we would be freed. We'd amble back to our neighborhood with our parents and our sisters and return to school.

Laying the spool at my feet, I wandered to the factory washroom. Even peeing felt healthy again. My body seemed to be able to cleanse instead of just consume itself.

"Things will be better now," I whispered.

I was very wrong.

Chapter 20

The End of Hope

Budzyn
Date uncertain

Staggered, my balance and equilibrium wavered, and then disappeared altogether. Gurgling was all I could hear, and after some indeterminate period I realized the guttural noises were coming from my own throat. Where was I? I was on a floor, but I didn't know where and why.

Opening my eyes, I discovered the answers. Standing on my hand, crushing my fingers, grinding my knuckles like a discarded cigarette, was a shiny black boot. A guard's boot. A boot that to me, lying on the floor trying desperately to recalibrate my bearings, seemed to belong to a being thirty feet tall.

There were commands in a language I did not understand, frantic but not loud. Hoisted to my knees, apparently by my shirt, I sat back against my calves and tried
to center myself, refocus, reestablish my senses. For what
seemed like hours but may have only been seconds, I was
allowed to recover. Finally, my eyes cleared. My thoughts
coalesced. The pain brought sudden clarity.

"*Mund*," the guard ordered. "*Mund*." His voice was a
whisper, but urgency crackled over the words.

A bony hand with nails creeping and curling over the
fingertips unbuttoned a holster. Removing the pistol, he
admired it, grinning, turning it over in his palm, leering
at it with reverence before straightening. He pressed the
barrel against my forehead. Was this the moment? Was a
bullet about to end my life? Countless heads punctured by
fatal wounds glared up in my memory. Was I about to be
just another? I could see myself, my forehead pierced, my
blood oozing from the orifice, my lifeless body crumpled
in a grotesque death pose.

"*Mund*," he whispered, his smile folding into a grimace.

"*Mund*," I said, having no idea what he was saying.

Grunting his disapproval, he ground the end of the
pistol into my skin.

The pistol was now below my chin, circling, then suddenly stopped at my lips. "*Mund*," he said again.

The barrel was inside my mouth, widening my lips and
jaw, clattering against my teeth, prying me open.

I closed my eyes and waited to hear the gun blast, but none came.

Cautiously, slowly, praying, I dared to move my eyelids, allowing only the tiniest of slits to peer through. What I saw confused me. His pants were lowered to his knees. His hips were trembling; his penis was gripped in his fingers.

The gun was gone, and he was clutching at the back of my head, wrenching me forward, his erection gagging me. Words spewed from him, groans, alternately expressing pleasure, then anger, then both at once. His movements quickened, less air became available, vomit rumbled in my esophagus. He wanted pleasure—his swaying was unmistakable—but he wanted me to suffer as well. Inserting himself with force, stopping, twisting me by the ears and temple, heaving me forward. The violence kept him enrapt; the gratification intertwined with the brutality quickened his pace.

The door to the washroom opened and two guards stepped inside, chatting as they entered. The man's movements halted and he stared at the intruders.

This will stop now, I thought.

The guards paused, studied us for a moment, turned, and departed, their conversation uninterrupted.

This disturbance only increased the fury. A careening fist across my cheek sent me sprawling, crashing against the wall, my neck compacting as my nose and skull bones flattened upon impact. Still, just as quickly, he was on me, raping me, sodomizing me, tying my filthy pants around my neck and leashing me to him.

I don't think I breathed until it was over.

Survival, I have learned, is tethered to hope. *Muselmanners* lost their hope, their will, their energy, everything. I imagine my parents must have lost hope. I think Pinia had also—if not when I told him there was nothing I could do to help us then when his father took his bread. I even believe some of the capos and guards were once decent people who had lost hope, and when they felt their life lurching into chaos could only then do what they did, witness what they witnessed, perpetrate the murders they did without compassion, let the world degenerate into madness they could control.

For what seemed now an eternity—for nearly as long as I could remember anyway—hope had clung to me, and I had clung to any kernel of hope that I could find. Through starvation, deprivation, filth, and unconscionable cruelty, somewhere deep within my soul I still had hope. Hope that my parents would find me; hope that Herzil would protect me; hope that I was strong enough to withstand the agony.

But now, as the guard came for me day after day, my optimism had for the first time waned.

His stench, his skin, so dry it was almost scaled, his filthy hair and wretched visage, attached themselves to me, and even after he was done, after he'd beaten me to near unconsciousness, abused me and covered me with his foulness, cursed at me and left me to wither, even after all that, his specter still hung close to me. I did not know it then but this shame was indelible. What did I do to warrant this? Why me and not some other child? Had I looked at him standing in the lines one day? These questions would haunt me forever.

Chapter 21

Heart Trouble

Boston

June 1983

The scars on my skin from the beatings they inflicted upon me, the tattooed number on my arm, the hoarding, the obsessive need to clean myself: These were effects of my past that anyone could easily diagnose. Even I understood the obvious, that these were the legacies of my childhood plain and in the open for everyone to see. But what wasn't quite so apparent were the wounds on the inside, the invisible wounds that were perhaps even more destructive but that no one could even imagine, especially me. Years of starvation as a child had altered my metabolism and made my body store calories in a manner that was, apparently, oddly haywire. This was exacerbated by my ever-present hunger, a by-product of the over-whelming fear of starvation I'd lived with for so long that left me the need to eat constantly and, too often, raven-ously. While this gorging gave my mind some short-term relief, inside, my body was deteriorating and faltering.

After I complained of being light-headed, it was a friend of mine who worked in health care who had to break the news to me.

"You need to see a cardiologist," Dr. Berger told me. "Quickly."

"But I am only fifty-two years old," I said. "My heart cannot be bad."

"You've suffered a lot, and for a long time, and some of these problems can start in childhood if nutrition is not maintained."

"I don't want to see any doctors. You tell me what to do. I trust you."

"If you trust me you will go today."

Awaiting surgery a few days later, I lay in my bed in the early hours of the morning and studying the scene around me. My children, asleep in chairs on opposite sides of my hospital bed, gave me comfort and made me realize that no matter what the outcome I at least had given something to the world to make it a better place. I listened to their soft breathing. For all my misfortune, I still had them. But what else did I have? Yes, I'd helped kids in Columbia Point and in the other projects, helped someone out of a bad situation here and there, but what had I really done? I'd witnessed the worst kind of hate, been subjected to irrational punishments for no reason, and endured hardships that no one should face, and I was mostly reluctant to speak of it unless I felt I had to, afraid of forcing people to confront what we often don't want to. To what purpose, I asked myself, was I shy about where I came from?

I studied my son Michael's face. He was deep in dreams.

I worried it could happen again—I still do, especially when I see the New England Holocaust Memorial targeted by vandals, as it was twice in the summer of 2017. People can be so cruel to one another, but this truth is something we all want to repress. We can so easily put the past behind us, dismiss the lessons to be learned to avoid the pain of understanding the suffering. I certainly wanted to myself.

Electronic noises came from the machines that were attached to me by wires and cords. My heart might give out at any moment, they had told me. The machines would make sure I stayed alive until the morning when they could operate on me. I wondered what would happen if they couldn't fix my heart. I needed to tell all the children I worked with what had happened to me. If everyone knew, we would have the tools next time to curb our cruelest, most vicious motives before it was too late.

I sat up in the bed. This is not going to take me, I vowed. There is so much to do, and because I survived I would need to complete the job for all my friends who didn't have the chance.

Chapter 22

Escape from Budzyn

Budzyn
Date uncertain

"Herzil, tomorrow, there will be a line after the morning count. Get in it—you and Szmulek."

Chapinski was whispering, standing near my brother, leaning toward him. Dazed and numb, I held the spool of wire and heard him speaking. His voice faded and rose, barely registered in my near oblivion.

"We'll be shot," Herzil stated.

"No, I have arranged this, with the other capos," he said.

"I don't trust them," Herzil said. "They will turn us in. Use us to gain favors. Turning us in will help them."

"Szmulek cannot endure much more, Herzil. You know

this. No food, now the beatings and whatever else. His eyes are telling me he is drifting away. The line is your only hope."

"When I get in the line, where does it take me?"

"To the train," Chapinski said.

"I took a train to get here to this place," Herzil replied. "Where will this train take us that is less dangerous than Budzyn?"

"Get on the train, Herzil. And take Szmulek. If you don't, soon this guard will kill him. He almost has three times already."

"And when this guard finds out you have arranged his departure, what will happen to you?"

"I intend to see you in Lodz when this is all finished," he said.

Chapter 23

Radom

Radom
Date uncertain

Why we were sent to Radom would soon become apparent. Chained by the legs, stilted in our steps, we hobbled
from the train and were paraded down the center of the
city, berated and spit upon by passersby, both civilian and
official, policemen in gray uniforms, SS officers, business-
men. There were perhaps thirty of us shuffling through
the dusty streets, and the level of contempt made me certain we had been sent to serve as examples. This is what
will happen if you disobey, was the message, I was certain.
You will be battered and starved and chained and made to

walk in prison lines through the streets, displayed to the public, humiliated and tortured.

But I was wrong. This was not why we had come. The scaffolds told me the reason. Scaffolds lined the streets block after block, turning around corners, disappearing and reemerging as we trudged on farther, scaffolds laden with the hanged. Men and women, elderly and children, some naked, others in tattered rags, their bodies limp and decaying, eyes open and lifeless, fifty to a block, their bones crumpling into themselves, weighing them down, corpses twisting and swaying, the ropes making strange friction noises against the wood to which they were tethered.

We had been sent here to replace the labor of the dead.

Had they all been hanged at once? I wondered.

"This is your new home," an SS officer announced outside the grim concrete fence, an open archway leading to a dim and crumpled village. "All Jews live inside here. Your work at the Fabryka Broni begins tomorrow. There will be exercises in the morning to ensure you are capable of working. If not, as these Jews were not"—he motioned to the swaying dead—"then not."

At my feet, the esplanade outside the gate leading to the ghetto was paved with Jewish headstones; headstones apparently stolen from Jewish cemeteries and cobbled into the earth replacing the cement or slate slabs that had once covered the pavement. We walked as if our feet were aflame, not wanting to disrespect the dead but having nowhere safe to step. Herzil, mouth agape, eyes filled with horror, turned from side to side as if he were searching for names he knew and stepping only where he saw monikers that were unfamiliar. Others tiptoed to avoid the Stars of David or the inscriptions, while others still seemed too tired or lost to even notice, the bodies strung up like rotting meat foreshadowing the fates to which they were now resigned.

Beyond the gate, through the archway, the ghetto of Radom sprawled in colorless gloom. A cloud of dust swirled and left a coating of dirt over everything it passed, and in the square several guards stood glaring out at passersby, most of whom seemed crippled or exhausted. Horses left untethered shuffled in place but even their movements seemed stilted, their rib cages protruding through their coats looking like the bones might break skin at any moment. Hassidic men, heads bowed and barely moving, slowly crossed between decrepit buildings, most wearing yellow armbands, many with canes or sticks supporting what little weight they had left. In the distance just at the edge of my vision a soldier with scissors tormented a man on his knees, the man's long black coat pulled back over his shoulders binding his arms as the soldier sliced at his beard and sideburns, a yarmulke blowing past his feet and out of sight. Children, too—some my age, some appearing younger though the lack of nourishment made it difficult to tell—squatted in the streets staring at us.

Most got bored after only minutes and soon went back to whatever games they were trying to play using stones and hats and tattered dolls. This was a camp, I realized. Just like Budzyn, though this was a prison within a city, an execution chamber in the dressings of a neighborhood.

Once inside we were freed and allowed to scatter.

"If you are found outside these gates, you will be shot," the SS officer called out as he departed. "Now mingle with the other vermin until we call you to calisthenics."

The Fabryka Broni, a plant on the outskirts of Radom, manufactured guns and ammunition. Word passed to everyone who worked there that the factory had been constructed around 1930, and that the VIS 35 pistol had become, over the following decade, the weapon of choice for soldiers fighting the Allies. The Reich equipped every soldier with the sidearm and as a result the fabrication of the handgun, which at the outset called for one twelve-hour shift, by now required that the operation run twenty-fours a day. Somehow Herzil and I got the day shift. It may have been that they'd executed so many of the other day workers that they needed us to fill in two of the vast number of empty posts left by the genocide. Or that they had simply stepped up production and needed more slave labor to meet the demand. Either way the conditions were grueling.

Herzil was again assigned to work on the electrical systems and the machinery, to keep the lights on and the forging equipment in good working order. I, together with dozens of other children and small groups of frail women, was assigned the grim task of filling shells with gunpowder. Painstaking, our job was fraught with perils. Black dust sifted through the air and coated our skin and lungs, and the crescendo of coughing during the day grew deafening. If chemicals got in our mouths, which they invariably did, the taste was so acrid, vomiting was commonplace. Nearly all the workers at these posts had buckets of their own swill at their feet, and because the air was dank already, the bile in the pails made the smell nearly intolerable. Most nerve-racking, however, was the danger. Guards with cigarettes passed by our small quarters, matches lit behind half-closed hands held to the smokes, and then passed from one to the other. Tiny sparks drifted to the floor. Everyone held their breath then. How explosions didn't blow us all to bits is a mystery I still can't solve.

True to the promise of the SS officer, before we were permitted to take the three-mile march to the factory each morning, and usually without the benefit of anything more than a cracker or plain broth, calisthenics were required. Marching in place, jumping jacks, and squats in the square inevitably led to an inmate collapsing or a too-loud complaint, and after that the offender was led off out the gate. Occasionally, the reverberations of a gun discharging would be heard not long thereafter, and even more frequently the dissenter's corpse would be identified swaying from the scaffolds as we passed on our way to Fabryka Broni. Despite the very public display of consequences, someone new always decided they'd had enough and could take no more.

But a new horror waited for me at Radom, a menace not only terrifying but even more inexplicable than anything that had come before. Somehow over the course of time I had come to expect cruelty, viciousness, and violence from the guards, the capos, the hired Ukrainian henchmen. I would never be prepared, however, for discovering children who were murderers.

Boys and girls, no older than I, filled with hate, overflowing with hostility, consumed with a desire to commit brutality to show their mentors their worth, populated the Radom factories.

"You are all ugly, oily monsters," a boy in a brown uniform screamed at us during calisthenics. The guard next to him laughed and held his shoulder. "Jew monsters and thieves."

He could not have been ten years old. In his uniform he seemed a miniature of the guard, who towered over him beaming with pride. Behind stood twenty more children, similarly dressed, all smiling, all at attention, all gleaming at the praise being showered upon them for hating us.

I scanned them from face to face, searching for some shred of understanding, some sympathy, even compassion, as if for a pet, or a doll, or a sibling. They didn't look at me. They had somehow learned that we—Jews—were tantamount to a lower form of life, or perhaps that we did not live at all.

"May I kick one?" the boy asked with excitement. "May I kick one in the head with my new boots?"

"Once the calisthenics begin, you will find one to try out your new boots," the guard replied, nodding his approval to the other guards standing nearby. "They've been taught well, eh?" he said, bemused.

The boy's boots rose to mid-thigh and were polished shiny and black. The toes were encased in steel, sharpened square edges gripping the instep. A girl in the line giggled.

My comprehension faltered. Dizziness welling up from inside me made me woozy. If I fell, would this boy beat me? I was his peer. He and I could have been friends; we could have chased trucks together, looked for sweets together, played the games I'd played in the yard.

"Running in place now," the guard shouted. "Everyone."

Our legs moved, heavy and tired.

"They aren't really doing it," the boy said. "That one is barely moving." He pointed to an elderly man who tried to pump his legs faster, both hands gripping his long beard to help his balance and to urge himself onward. The man's eyes bulged with fear.

"That is pitiful," the boy said.

This boy looks like Pinia, I thought. Pinia wouldn't hurt anyone.

The other uniformed children murmured with excitement.

The elderly man stumbled, then tried to right himself before exhaustion tangled his legs and he sprawled to the concrete. He rose to a crawling position and lifted his head imploringly to the guard.

Barely moving his eyes, the guard motioned to a sentry nearby who removed a pistol from its holster, flipped it in his hand, and brought the grip down angrily upon the elderly man's shoulder. He collapsed.

A pounding reverberated in my heart. I stopped running in place. Everyone did.

"May I kill it now with my boots," the boy asked the guard.

The guard nodded.

Head raised and arms crossed, the boy marched in rhythmic steps to the fallen man. The first kick was tentative, as if he was testing the man's firmness and his own resolve. No one else moved and not a sound could be heard. He kicked again, this time against the man's temple. The man gasped and tried to cover his head. The boy kicked harder, his method and approach and leverage improving with each swing of his leg.

"You must move your arms for me to kick you properly," the boy screeched.

The elderly man did not move.

Another boy walked from the group, slightly older and

taller than the first. He pulled at the edges of his perfectly pressed shirt. His first kick broke the elderly man's arm, which bent between the elbow and shoulder at an impossible angle. Mouth agape, the elderly man seemed about to scream with agony. He was stopped by the first boy's boot crashing against his jaw.

Together they beat the elderly man, alternating their leg swings until they seemed to move as a single unit.

"He's dead," the guard finally said, raising his hands to tell them to stop.

The elderly man was pulp and nothing more. His face had no form and blood pooled out around him in a jagged circle before finding a rivulet in the concrete and running in a stream away from the corpse.

"My pants," the younger boy cried out. Below his knee, blood was spattered over the fabric. "He has made me filthy," he stammered. Another kick followed and the elderly man's body rolled over, his dead arm slapping the ground.

"Enough calisthenics," the guard said, turning back to us. "Double line. Go."

Chapter 24

No Matter How Bad

South Boston High School
April 1984

The podium and the microphone didn't feel right. What I wanted to say needed my unmagnified voice; the sound of my ordeal had to resonate without a filter. If I was to explain what had happened to me, it had to be genuine, intimate, no special effects. I came off the stage and stood just feet from the front row of the auditorium.

"What is with the clown suit, mister," someone shouted from the back.

A dull laughter percolated through the cavernous room with a bit of unease, as I knew some of them knew. I waited, pulling the cap down farther until it covered my temples. I buttoned the tattered gray prison blouse to the top.

"These are the clothes I wore for six years," I said. "In ten concentration camps." I paused. "Ten camps. Do you know what *concentration camp* means?"

The giggling stopped.

"Not clothes like these," I continued. "These exact rags. That was all they gave me for six years. I worked in these clothes. I slept in these clothes and watched thousands of people die in these clothes. Children, mothers, teenagers just like you. Right in front of me. I watched all that happen in these clothes.

"Do you know what happened? Have you read about what my family and friends all endured—what took all of them away from me—in the camps where the Nazis put us?"

No one spoke.

"I am not here to give you a history lesson. You can read about that. Your teachers can tell you. They can show you the pictures. Maybe some of you have seen them."

I told them that I was there to show that if I could survive what happened to me, and make something of my life here in America, then so could any of them, no matter what they were up against. "I know that many people grow up with problems at home," I said, "and that it can be tempting to think you're better off making money in the streets than anywhere else, but I am telling you that is not the way. School is the way. Education is the way. I came here with nothing. I came here after being beaten so many times I stopped trying to count. I lost my family when I was eight years old. I was completely alone. But people told me if you want to live in America and be part of America, you have to be determined to learn. You have to study. You have to stay in school and listen to your teachers and not go out to the streets."

I paused to scan the room to see if the students were listening. The auditorium was still.

"I lived in these shitty clothes for six years," I said, pulling at the striped gray blouse. "Look at these! I had no choice. If I took them off I would get shot. I stole a potato once, I was so hungry I didn't care what happened to me. They beat me with rifles and until I was bleeding and swollen. I was a child; still they hit me with their fists and their guns. Why they didn't kill me I didn't know until recently. Now I know."

I could feel the stares. I could almost feel their hearts beating.

"They didn't kill me because I needed to come here to tell you these things. This is why I am still on this earth. To be here."

And it was. In the months since my heart problems were diagnosed, I'd started spreading my story widely, reminding students that they weren't alone in struggling and there were people here to help.

I took off my hat.

"After I got here, after the long journey, the orphanages, the displacement centers, after everything that happened, a doctor told me: Here in America there is opportunity but you have to take it. And you take it through school. Stay in school, he said. Do your learning and you can be a success and overcome all the hardships. And I listened to him. I went to school. I slept in cars when I didn't have a house just so I could get to school. I took jobs to pay for it. I did whatever I had to do to get an education. And now because of that I can help you. In fact, it's my job to help you. Ask me for my help. I can help you no matter how bad you think your life is. Let me help you."

When I finished the principal shook my hand and murmuring began to filter across the room.

"Let me know what you think of my talk," I said to him.

"I don't have to," he answered. "There has never been an assembly like this. They rarely listen to anyone. Please keep doing this in as many places as you can."

Chapter 25

The Honor of Work

Radom

Date uncertain

My survival was dependent on some inner strength that I could not fully articulate, even in my own my mind, and that I doubted nearly constantly. I couldn't take another step, another day of this work, a single more murder. Let them take me, hang me up on the scaffolds, take Herzil by the hand and lead him to the Germans to be shot, both of us together. The agony will stop.

The thoughts would come to me and circle in my head, but just as soon be dismissed. Still, the idea of holding my own fate in my hands may have been what gave me strength. The idea of not letting them control what happened to me ultimately was strangely comforting and pushed me onward. I am so much stronger than any of you soldiers, I began to say in my head. They have the guns, the power, the anger, the means, and yet somehow I have the control.

So I went on.

Months passed. We worked, slaved, did our exercises, and quietly filed in our lines to the factories and back. Many died, the same way others had died before them, collapsing in the street, kicked or beaten to death, starved, hanged, some just disappearing, never to be seen again. New prisoners came as well. A group of Romany arrived from a camp they thought was somewhere near the border of France. A smaller group of Polish intellectuals, non-Jews, seemed suddenly just to settle with us as if they'd come from thin air or some backdoor entrance no one knew about. They had their own shelter, away from us, but like us, every morning they did the calisthenics then marched off to the plant, most usually begging the guards to free them. "I am not Jewish. My family, they are all Catholics. Please, can we speak to someone. Our being here is a mistake."

The guards did not care. Jews, Romany, homosexuals, even Germans who did not look Aryan enough were abandoned to work and suffer. All of us were "other." Not them, not whatever the guards thought they were that separated them from us—whatever they were or thought they were. Soon they will become suspicious of each other, Herzil said. In the meantime they will just be crueler and crueler.

"If you are fit enough, you will have the honor of being put to work mining the material to build Germania, the new world, the shining civilization on the hill," a new German captain announced one morning. "This is work that you shall be proud of, I assure you." He paced up and down the lines of prisoners in formation to do the morning exercises. "Albert Speer has formulated a new vision for our people, how we are to live, what our cities should look like, what a community for those graced by the will of God to be of Aryan descent should look like and how it should function, and it is my job to commence the process of gathering the fine granite to make this vision a reality." He stopped. "And while of course you will never live in such a place, you will at least have the benefit of knowing you helped to create it in a small way.

"Only those who are strong and vital will be allowed to touch these materials, however. We want no near-dead Jewish stink on these fine stones."

Signaling to another younger guard, the captain gestured to get the lines moving. "Get them to the train," he said.

"You will be going to Auschwitz now, stopping for a short visit before continuing to the quarry.

"Take them. Go."

*　　*　　*

Uncertainty and endless waiting made our existence excruciating, and there seemed to always be a selection process, a contest of fitness that reminded us of our weakness while filling us with trepidation. Every time it felt as though the end was just one wrong glance or one wayward cough away.

"If you are too weak to walk the extra miles to the trains, we have carts and wagons in which we can transport you," the younger guard bellowed.

He was blond and just about my age. His face was chiseled, structured in a near-perfect triangle, his chin jutting, his cheeks wide, his eyes a glistening green. He looked so young and innocent, you could almost imagine that he actually wanted to be helpful.

Scores shouted out, raised their arms, or turned to him and stepped out of the line. Some were older, some weak in the legs, others just tired. "Please, I will ride in the wagon. My feet, my legs, a rest will be good for them."

I watched fearfully, knowing that to take respite in the carts was tantamount to suicide. I wanted to scream out to them, warn them, go on a diatribe informing them they were foolish, naive, stupid even, to believe these guards after all we'd seen and witnessed. *How can you? Why would you? What reasons are there?*

But I said nothing. I let these people feed the Nazis'

endless lust for our blood, let them sacrifice themselves. I live every day of my life knowing that I watched it happen.

Snaking toward the outward roads leading east of the ghetto, our column trailed dust and despair behind us. No one turned—no one even flinched—when the shots rang out in the distance, a withering scream dying in the morning air.

The empty wagons joined us at the train.

Chapter 26

The Train to Auschwitz

Location uncertain
Date uncertain

There seemed to be thousands of us packed into a single railcar. The more bodies the Germans could crowd into a single car, the more cars they had left to transport goods to wherever the war effort needed them. As a result, we were left with no room to sit and rest our legs, forced to hold ourselves upright, barely able to turn in place for fear of stepping on a foot or crushing a child too small to notice in the chase.

Inevitably, legs gave way and bodies collapsed, muscles going limp with exhaustion. Groans echoed when someone went down; not sounds of sympathy but sounds of inconvenience, disturbance, annoyance. Somehow the crumpled bodies would be pushed or kicked across the floorboards, discarded, dead or alive, against the edge of the locked doorways.

At the end of the second day, just as dawn began to seep through the ragged edges of the boards lining the car, the train slowed. A mass of bodies pressed against me as it lurched to a stop.

Discussions erupted from every corner of the car. "Why have we stopped," some shouted with worry. "Please let us out to stretch."

The smell of urine and feces was everywhere. Having nowhere to move, people went where they stood, and now that we were no longer moving the air grew still.

"Be still," someone near me moaned. "They have to let us out soon. They would shoot us if they wanted us dead. Be still."

One hour passed, then two, then more than I could keep track of.

"Out. Now. Push the bodies to the ground."

The doors were opened, and I could see that it was dusk. Once the door slid back, bodies tumbled and fell to the earth, the dead first. Guards shouted instructions, but there seemed to be more prisoners streaming from the trains than the guards could handle amid the rising commotion. Still, those who were there had their rifles poised.

"Children there, adults in this line," a guard screeched as we tumbled forward.

I studied the scene before me.

Children were standing off to one side crying, arms outstretched, reaching across the air toward their parents, guards shoving them back if they breached the barrier between the queues. Siblings held on to one another, dragging out this final moment together.

At the front of that line was a teetering table where prisoners were made to sit and extend their forearms toward a grim woman who worked fervently. She pressed her needled counter into each arm until they bled then rubbed black ink into the wounds. Before the next prisoner approached she quickly interchanged the number then pressed again. Everyone got a number except for the frail, who were ominously told to wait together behind the last car. A few moments later they were blocked from my view, and I knew how their story would end.

A guard shoved me with his gun toward the children's line.

Seeing the infirm shuttled away to what could only be their deaths without first getting tattooed on their arms, I became fixated on somehow getting a number. If they would mark my arm, give me the identity of a number, subhuman though it was, I believed it would somehow aid my survival. I reasoned that it was the only way and that if I was discarded later, there would at least be a trace left behind of what had happened to me.

A woman collapsed and as heads turned, I dodged the

guard and pushed my way between two men in the adult line. For an instant they seemed about to protest; then they shrugged and their heads drooped. I waited, trying somehow to make myself big and small simultaneously. I trudged along with the line.

Chapter 27

How I Learned of Robert Hall

Old Harbor Development, Boston
September 4, 1967

The Old Harbor Development covers a large triangle of land surrounded by Old Colony Avenue, Preble Street, Dorchester Avenue, and the railroad tracks. Whitey Bulger, the notorious Boston crime boss, was raised in Old Harbor and though it was constructed in 1938, little had changed by the time I was sent there, tasked with motivating the neighborhood's teenagers to return to school.

It was the summer, and with school out and jobs scarce many of the teenagers had little to do. There was lots of public drinking, daily fistfights.

I admired the police and the hard work they did, but when they finally decided to go undercover and infiltrate the neighborhood to figure out what to do, their efforts were woeful. Cops dressed as the hippies of the era with long hair flowing, dungaree jackets, and sandals would be outed as soon as they opened their mouths. I decided to take a different approach.

"He ain't no cop," someone said as I approached a group standing outside a basketball court in one of my early experiments in the neighborhood.

"Nope," another replied. "But who the hell is he?"

Another boy answered—I couldn't catch what he said—and soon they were all laughing.

I was dressed as I always was, plain blue slacks and pale-gray shirt. A dozen or so kids were sitting in the shade, some shirtless, others in sweat-drenched tees. They'd apparently just walked off the court behind them, which I noticed had but one crooked basketball hoop, dust swirling up and across it from a dry breeze.

"The last guy had us running for cigarettes and washing his car. We told him to fuck off and he ran away. So what do you want?"

"Which one of you is the basketball player?"

They glanced at each other but no one spoke.

"I'm looking for Brian Wallace," I said. I pointed at a boy who, though he was seated, looked long and lanky.

"What's with the accent?" a kid with disheveled red hair asked. "You German or something?"

"I was born in Poland," I said. "I am definitely not German."

One of the boys nodded to me. "I'm Brian Wallace. Why do you want to know?"

"You are the basketball player?" I said. "Aren't basketball players supposed to be tall?"

"How do you know me?" Wallace asked. He wrinkled his nose and spat, as if to tell me not to push him.

"Do you know Frankie Pederson?"

Wallace nodded.

"I work with Frankie, and he told me to ask for you. He said you were a good kid and would help me."

"Help you do what?" he asked. His friends chuckled.

"I am your new youth worker," I said.

"Get the fuck out of here," one of the boys said. He was turned away from me, sitting behind his friends. "You are about a hundred years old. I'll bet you need someone to help you wipe your own ass."

Everyone laughed. The laughter didn't bother me, as I could tell I was close to making progress.

"What is your name?" I asked the boy who had commented about my age.

"My name is Jimmy. What is it to you?" he answered.

"Jimmy what?" I persisted.

"What, are you writing a book? Why don't you kiss my ass and make it a love story." The boy's audience cheered.

"No, Jimmy, I am here to help you. Now, what is your last name?"

"Davis," he said, a bit less sure of himself.

I asked him about himself, asked his friends what they did for fun. Eventually, I steered the discussion to the importance of education for giving them the freedom to do what they wanted with their lives. I must have jumped in too quickly because one of the boys soon interrupted me to ask about my clothes.

"Where did you get these pants?" he said. "Robert Hall?"

"What do you mean?"

"Robert threw them out, and you hauled them in." They all laughed. I found out later that Robert Hall was a local clothing store.

I laughed along with them. "Are they that bad?" I asked.

"They do suck," Jimmy said. He was smirking.

I extended my hand to the little basketball player, who shook it a little too hard.

"I have a feeling that a lot of people underestimate both of us," I said. "I'm Steve. Steve Ross."

"The oldest youth worker in Boston," Jimmy said.

"Do you think you are tall enough to play for the Celtics?" I asked Brian.

"Probably not, but a lot of coaches really like the way I play," he said.

"Good for you. I am proud of you. But if you can't play for the Celtics, why don't you own the Celtics?"

He sneered. "How the hell would a kid like me ever own the Celtics?"

"I don't know if you *will* ever own the Celtics," I conceded. "But maybe, who knows, with a college degree and some luck, you just might."

"A college degree?" he said, turning to his friends, who laughed.

"A college degree," I said.

The boys got quiet. A gust of wind offered some relief from the heat.

"No one we know goes to college," he finally said. "No one around here can afford it. We mostly have to fend for ourselves."

"Okay. Well, maybe that is about to change."

"Bullshit," Jimmy said. "The army, that is the only way out of here, and that only gets you into a body bag."

I rose from the seat I'd taken on the cold concrete sidewalk. "I am coming here next Saturday," I said. "The college boards, the entrance exams, are being held at Boston College High School that morning. I will drive you there. I've already arranged for you to take the test for free. You just have to show up and take the test."

"I just told you, no one can afford college. Why would we take the stupid test?" Jimmy said.

"I'll take care of that also," I said. "If you take the

test and get into a college, I will figure out how it gets paid for."

Again their faces betrayed doubt. This time, however, it was mixed with confusion.

On Saturday six of them were sitting under the tree near the court when I arrived. Money immediately exchanged hands among them with slaps into palms.

"Damn, he came," one boy said, paying up on the bet he'd made.

"Let's go," I said.

I dropped them at Boston College High School and my heart filled up with pride. They seemed eager and ready and I watched them file into the building warily eyeing the affluent kids who moved about as if they belonged, a feeling my kids surely did not have.

Driving back toward Old Harbor to see what else I could do that morning, I thought about my parents and my family, and Pinia, and wondered what they would think about me. I remembered kissing my father's beard when he praised me, and hugging my mother and sisters when they said I was going to find greatness. I remembered Pinia's bold pronouncements about my future. I could feel their presence, their warmth, their joy, could almost hear them all.

The next day I returned to find them.

"So how did it go?" I asked.

"They were hard, man," Jimmy said, shifting as he spoke.

"*Really?*" I said, staring. "I have trouble believing that."

"What do you mean?"

"You were all back in Southie before the test even started," I said. "Why? Do you think this is a game? Do you think I am fooling with you? Did you think that was funny? Do you want to be living in the projects when you're a hundred years old like me?"

None of them would look at me.

"People are trying to help you, and you spit on their hand. I wish I had the opportunities you have."

I turned my forearm into view. "I know you know what that is," I said. "You know what it means to me?" I tugged at my hair in frustration. "It means I know what generosity is. I had my life saved dozens of times by people who had less than any of you will have at the lowest point of your life. People who owed me nothing gave me water to save my life, and it's in part because I was grateful for it. I know what generosity is and when it isn't worth the effort."

They were quiet for a minute, studying their feet. "Come on, man," someone finally said. "You beat the Nazis, but you can't beat a bunch of project kids? We thought you were tougher than that."

"We were just busting your balls," Jimmy said.

"Are they giving the test again?" one of them asked.

"Do you want me to drive you?" I asked.

"Hell no, we are never getting in that shit box again," one of them said. "It's bad for our reputations."

"We'll steal a car," Jimmy said.

"You will not," I yelled.

The boy was beaming. "Oh man, I got you good."

Chapter 28

Tattooed

148127. I looked at my arm, then at the woman who'd
marked me sitting with her needles and ink. She grinned
and rolled her eyes to tell me to move on. I had been
marked. My existence reduced to a series of figures.

There was a count beginning, and my pulse began to
race. There had been a count as soon as the adult line
was formed, before I'd escaped into it. It seemed certain I
would be found out. Or worse, if I wasn't found out they
would do what they always did: put us all in a line, make
someone confess to being one of the sick ones trying to
deceive them, trying to get in a line where they didn't

belong. Someone would get shot, probably more than one person if no one would admit they'd gotten a number or gotten in a line where they didn't belong.

I reasoned with myself to stay quiet. But there was another voice as well, urging me to give myself up.

"Single file, back on the trains," a guard said. "Only those with numbers. Children and those in the line to the left remain here, where you'll be fed and housed."

"No talking," another guard shouted.

People began to move. Children wept and reached for their parents. The noise—shrieking, crying, praying— was deafening. I moved with the lines, looking back at the kids being left behind.

The count that was going to be off continued.

The train whistles blew. Steam seemed to pour out from under the wheels. I turned from side to side. My heart felt like it might explode.

"My count is three hundred forty-eight," a guard screamed, pushing the last of a line of men into a car.

"Two hundred thirty-three," another announced of a different line.

I watched the guard adding up the numbers on a clipboard, thoughts crashing through my head. Should I shout a distraction, grab the clipboard, anything to make him lose count? I realized those were only temporary answers, since he would go back and recount if he was distracted. He'd start again, add the numbers, and someone would die. All because I simply wanted to survive and slipped into the group that I thought would let me.

I studied the Ukrainian guards at the trains. Their black-and-yellow uniforms were disheveled and dirty. One had a fresh scar across his cheek still oozing fluid. His cigarette hung from his lips and ashes dropped on his arms and the gun's barrel. Another mumbled under his breath, smiled for a second, then kicked at the ground. They argued. I could only assume it was over the inconsistent counts they'd gotten.

There was something in this encounter that made me pause and listen and watch more carefully. Something was creating an energy inside me that both nagged at me and made me more certain I needed to keep studying them.

The smell of the cigarettes reminded me of the night I'd ventured out with my mother in Krasnik, searching for food. The Ukrainian guards who'd approached us had only been foreshadowed by the scent of smoke. Had we been caught we would have been shot, but we weren't. I had stood still and silent inside the train car where we'd found potatoes and, hiding behind a barrel, my mother had wedged herself under the car, balanced somehow on the axles.

That's when I knew what to do. I watched the guards dispute, looking for an opening. Their gesturing and inflections became more intense. One man turned to face the other, his head still down as he stamped out a cigarette butt. This was the best moment I would get.

I darted behind them as a train whistle blasted. Slipping under and behind a wheel, I waited, trying not to breathe. The whistle was long and wailing and several more followed from other trains in the distance. I could hear the guards still scuffling.

I allowed myself to raise my head, to study the undercarriage. An axle was near my face, black grease spread and clumping near the enormous metal wheels. A latticework of metal bars crisscrossed the wooden floor above me. There was a chance I could squeeze through the two bars that seemed the most evenly separated, but I worried they might creak. The guards' boots were so close in front of me I could reach out and touch them.

"Get these rats into the train," an officer barked. The boots moved away, shuffling over to a line of prisoners gathered nearby. I could see the withered legs of the men they were prodding to move toward the train door. Blood stained nearly all of their pant legs, in one area or another. They were each hobbled by a different limp.

"Move," the guards commanded.

Their voices were my cue. I lifted myself as quietly as I could, suppressing the grunts of my effort to combat the weakness I felt in my arms. Pressing my face into the wooden floorboards, I dragged my torso through the upper bars until my shoulders were balanced on the latticework. My legs followed, and I wedged them into the tiny space nearest the axle. My foot twisted when I made the last push to lift myself off the ground, and pain shot though my hips and knees. My cheek, still flush against the wood, began to ooze blood, as if I'd scraped myself with sharp claws.

My arms began to go numb, the blood cut off by my odd position, and I tried to shift as quietly as I could to restore blood flow. How long I could remain in this spot, perched precariously three feet off the ground, I didn't know, nor did I have a clue what would happen to the lat-ticework around me once the train began to move. Would going around a curve throw everything askew? Was I going to get dumped back down on the track, sliced in two by the wheels as they rumbled forward?

I marveled at the determination of my mother years ago. Perhaps she, too, was out there under a train now, holding on for her life. I could hardly contemplate the alternative.

The train lurched forward. The startling movement nearly toppled me but I caught myself with one arm. The arm was still tingling, but I knew I had no option except to hold on. I grabbed at whatever I could to steady myself. Imperfections in the track made the wheels bounce, and my body flailed with the movements.

I have to let go, I thought.

But I pulled myself up and twisted, freeing my arm and curling my legs around the bar closest to the wheels to relieve the pressure on my abdomen. Dust and stones kicked up and pelted my eyes and cheeks, but I covered my head with an elbow and focused on the floor above me. It creaked with the tiny movements of the men crowded inside. The boards bowed occasionally and pressed into my temple, but I convinced myself they wouldn't break and crush my head. Why I was so sure I didn't know. I was sure because I had to be.

Within half an hour the train was moving at a steady pace, and the bumps threw me harder, retesting my grip.

I closed my eyes and thought about Lodz, about my mother and my sisters and Rosh Hashanah dinners and playing cards in the yard with my friends. I thought about Herzil and my grandmother, and all the beautiful things we would do if we could all be together again.

Darkness had set in by the time the train slowed and jolted me from my reveries. I had no plan for how I could reintegrate myself as a prisoner, and if I tried to jump from the slowing train and escape, my Nazi-issued pajama uniform and emaciated appearance would immediately give me away.

I would have to find a way to quietly descend from my perch, roll off the track, and get in the lines, all without being seen by either the guards or the prisoners. We prisoners may have been in the same boat, but one of the tragedies of the Holocaust was how successfully the Nazis managed to use carrots and sticks to divide us. If one of my comrades saw me he or she might gape or gasp, but

Current Check-Outs summary for KRELIK, D
Thu May 16 11:56:54 EDT 2019

BARCODE: 33036112707380
TITLE: From broken glass : my story of f
DUE DATE: Jun 06 2019

even worse, the prisoner might turn me in hoping to gain favor with the guards.

The train staggered to a stop, smoke seeping out below the car and choking me. An eerie quiet descended. I could still hear the prisoners shuffling about above me, but beyond the car there were none of the noises I expected. Every camp I'd ever been to had come with its own chaos of sounds—wailing in the night, praying for God to intervene, the barked commands of guards.

The train car door above me swung open, and I could see the disheveled legs of the prisoners flash two by two as they stepped, quivering, down.

I tried to quiet my breathing, listening to hear the count.

"You—stay where you are," I heard. I worried I had been caught.

When nobody came to pull me from the car, I understood it was directed at others.

I shimmied free of the bars and lowered myself onto the track. A trickle of blood from where my cheek had been pressed against the floor dripped onto the stones below me. I crouched then inched forward until the backs of the legs of the prisoners were before me, and in one quick motion I pushed up and joined the line, glancing side-to-side to see if I was to be exposed.

Three prisoners studied me quizzically.

"I had to pee," I said, pointing under the train. I shrugged. I held my breath. "I had to pee."

One rolled his eyes at me before looking away. "Piss in your pants next time," he said. "You'll get us all killed."

It turned out that the transit camp in Bietighiem had been empty. I was relieved to know we weren't being led to an execution line in the forest—or we probably weren't. Barbed-wire fencing surrounded the barracks as it had all the other camps I'd been to, but outside the wire walls the landscape looked different. Rolling hills and an aqueduct crossed the far reaches of the distance surrounding the camp. Sprinkled along the roads were houses and buildings and structures that seemed untouched by the war. Local people milled about and seemed to ignore the fencing and the barracks. The children playing outside the gate didn't so much as turn to look at us.

Inside the fence, the barracks were lined up in rows as they had been in other camps, and the construction materials seemed identical to Budzyn and Radom. Two of the structures, however, seemed to have burned to the ground, leaving behind only ash-crusted rubble to testify to what had been. How this could have happened troubled me—there was no system inside the camps that could catch fire, no fireplaces for warmth, no kitchens or electricity.

What horrors had happened here?

Chapter 29

Matriculation

Brandeis University
1967

"What can I do for you, Mr. Ross?" the admissions officer said. "I understand you needed to have my ear and you would stop at nothing to get it." Brandeis University is a prominent college just outside Boston. The office smelled of leather and dust, like a forgotten section of a library.

I smiled. "It's true," I said. "I came here to ask you an important question, and I appreciate you taking the meeting." I studied the two portraits of former deans that flanked his desk. "You have an amazing program here," I added. "Many of them. All filled with some of the most talented students anywhere. But I have one question about them. I need to know how many students come here from the city schools in South Boston."

He adjusted in his seat, smoothing the wrinkles in his pants with his palms. "It's a good question, but I don't know exactly. I'd have to check and get back to you."

I paused and inhaled the scent of leather. "Okay. Well then, I should tell you something. That was a trick question. I actually know the answer. And it's zero."

He shook his head no. "That cannot be right."

"It is," I said. "We keep close records on where our graduates end up among the Boston schools. And having seen them, I can tell you there is not a single one."

"You do understand, Mr. Ross, that the qualifications to come to Brandeis are—"

"I am well aware of the qualifications, sir. But you should be aware that there are many very smart children in the city who never get a chance." I leveled with him, explaining that he was not the problem; Brandeis was not intending to exclude the boys and girls I worked with. "The issue is," I said, "that there are no programs to help them get to places like this. They do not feel welcomed here and so they don't even attempt to come here."

"We—we are very open to them coming." There was a tightness in his jaw that I hadn't noticed before. "As you know, they must have the grades; they must have taken the college entrance exam; they must submit their application for the committee's review."

I said that I had taken them to the college entrance exam myself and had the fees waived to pay for it.

"I'll need to discuss with the committee what could be done," he said, clearing his throat.

"You, sir, have the power to make a difference, to take a stand and make this decision." I looked down at my lap and noticed my fists were clenched. I tried to even my breaths, though I could feel my anger rising.

"Here is what I can do," I finally told him. "I will bring you six qualified students, and you will let them take summer school classes here. On a scholarship. If they are successful, you can enroll them in school here and either pay for their tuition or provide them with aid tied to a job here on campus."

He rose from his seat and thanked me for coming, extending a hand. "I need to discuss this with my colleagues," he said.

I rose as well and took his hand. I knew how to push, but I also knew when my time was up.

"One thing that I think you ought to mention with them is that I have already met with Boston College, Harvard, and Northeastern, who are each taking six city students. I'm working with a journalist at the *Boston Globe* about a feature on this enrollment crisis. I suggest you make your decision soon, he being under a deadline and all."

I knew exactly what I was doing, and I had no misgivings whatsoever using the power of bad press in this way.

"How will we know who to pick?" he said, and I knew in that moment that I'd cut through.

"Here are your students," I said, passing papers across his desk. "Their grades and test scores are all there.

"I think you'll like Mikey Glynn and Paul Regan a lot. Mikey wants to be a social worker, and Paul wants to be a lawyer."

Chapter 30

An Empire Falls

Dachau

Date uncertain

How I got to Dachau, I could not remember. Something had finally broken inside me, and as the rest of my body struggled so did my memory. I worried that my heart was beating a little faster every day and my lungs slowing, both trying desperately to compensate for the lack of nourishment.

I remember the camps I went to next only in flashes—the cold barracks I was shuttled into, the cycling onto and off of trains. I came to learn later—through the records I found—that I had passed through Vaihingen, Bettingen-Stuttgart, Gross-Sachsenheim, Bietigheim, Unterriexingen, and Neckar-Els before I finally landed at Dachau, the one that I remember most vividly.

Though we prisoners didn't know it, the war had turned decidedly against the Germans by the time I was living in Dachau, and the prospect of losing altered the levels of the guards' cruelty. Something happens to people when they are forced to confront that they have committed heinous and unconscionable crimes; the prospect of exposure turns them even more malicious as nihilism and fear overtake them.

Dachau itself was a mixture of filth and stink. The latrines were in disrepair and alternately overflowed and oozed waste out into the yards—it mattered little as many had lost control of their functions and rarely made it to the latrines in the first place.

The barracks were also crumbling. Roofs fell in on rafters, walls collapsed, and the three- or four-level bunks that served as beds fell one upon the other regularly, usually crushing people left beneath them who screamed in agony until they finally went quiet. The floors had also begun to disintegrate, leaving large ragged holes of splintered wood that dazed prisoners often fell through, sometimes earning gashes that would kill them given the lack of treatment.

The images sometimes come back to me even now when I least expect it. A rope snapping tight in one of the random hangings they performed at the towers; an infant being taken from its mother and hurled alive onto a mass grave; bloodshot eyes staring back at me from the dark corners of the barracks—all these images loom at me in feverish nightmares. The triggers might be an ache in my chest or a pang of hunger, and they will send me spiraling into dread and memory, as if a part of me is still at Dachau, unable to leave.

Chapter 31

Dead, Gone, and Forgotten

Dachau

Date uncertain

I learned that starvation eventually brings numbness. After days with nothing to eat, the mind goes quiet, nerves stop firing, temperature is irrelevant, and breathing no longer feels automatic, as if you actually have to think about opening your diaphragm like you would open your fist. There were several moments I remember at Dachau when I consciously thought I should just stop.

I do not remember how I made it from the yard into the guardhouse, but somehow—for some reason—I did. There, I found that even the guards' barrack was in disrepair, a further offshoot of the deteriorating conditions of the war for the Germans. Paint was chipped and littered on the floor; several of the windows were webbed with cracks and others shattered, pools of brown water gathering underneath.

The potato I found in a dusty corner looked to me like a globe. It was round and moist and glistened and the skin seemed to me to all earth and chocolate at once. I remembered the soil at the farm where my mother had left me and wondered whether this beautiful orb had been grown there in the deep black dirt I'd run my hands through. There was nothing else in the world at the moment I held it, no camp, no guards, no disease, no death. It seemed at that moment to be a miracle, like the eight nights the oil lasted at the Temple, like the Red Sea parting, or like God providing manna.

I wrapped my shaking fingers around the sandy surface. It felt cool to the touch, but also oddly electric. Its flavor flooded onto my tongue, as if my hand could somehow taste it. Saliva filled the space under my tongue and spilled into my cheeks. My eyes closed with the sensation and all my senses fired at once. Air filled my lungs.

Letting my eyes fall open, I dropped my prize into my pocket.

A rifle butt slammed into my nose, and I saw a tooth spit out from between my lips and a string of blood followed it as if they were connected. The ceiling came into view next and my neck bent back in an arc that was followed by my arms, then my torso, and finally my flailing legs. I'd been hit so hard that the spin was stopped only by my face hitting the floor after I'd flipped across the room. A cloudy gray then descended over my eyes, which became red, then yellow stars. I glimpsed the potato rolling across the floor, the distance from my hand increasing with each turn.

I should have known that they weren't finished. Boots swung at my face and belly, one striking my hip so hard I felt the socket give way and bones lurch out of place. The steel toe that hit my chest made the air rush out of me. One soldier continued to hammer my face and neck with the rifle stock; another pistol-whipped my arms and shoulders, my face out of his reach.

I remember a fist at one point squeezing around my testicles until I nearly fainted.

"Fucking scum," one of them seethed at me. "You should all die."

"He's dead now," another growled.

"Good, put him with the others to be burned later."

"Take him," a guard said.

With a grip on my bloody blouse another guard lifted me easily off the floor and threw me toward the doorway. I crumpled against the frame and lay as still as I could, trying to breathe but quietly and without movement.

"Once he's in the pile, burn them," the guard said.

I was lifted onto a stretcher and carried, my hands and

feet dragging across the dirt as the two guards supporting me walked. When they reached the pile of corpses
they paused for a moment. They knew I wasn't dead, and
their movements seemed confused as they spoke quietly.
I still wonder today if it was a moment of indecision I
observed, as if in the depths of their corruption a voice
asked if they could truly throw a living child into a pile
to be burned alive.

Then they launched me onto the tangled mound of
bodies.

Chapter 32

The Busing Crisis

South Boston
November 13, 1974

Why people treat each other the way they do, I will never understand.

Busing came to South Boston in 1974. A federal judge had stood up to the city's public schools being segregated. Schools that were predominantly black were going to have white children bused to attend classes, and black children would be bused to schools that had previously been mostly white.

What was a reasonable solution to an unequal and unjust situation for children that had festered for too long quickly turned deadly. Parents were furious that their children would be forced into schools that were sometimes underperforming, and instead of blaming school administrators they blamed the children who looked different from their own.

At first parents simply refused to put their children on the buses; even those children who were to remain at the same school were kept home in protest. Less than a third of the enrollment at South Boston High School attended school once busing commenced, and those who did attend found the police presence overwhelming.

Then the protestors attacked several black students and the community erupted in violence.

South Boston High School was closed for a month after a stabbing on its campus, and clashes between its white and black students had become so prevalent that even after its reopening metal detectors were installed at every entrance. Racially motivated incidents continued on an almost daily basis, and in one a man was nearly beaten to death after being pulled from his car.

The racial violence transported me back to the childhood that similar ethnic prejudices had taken away from me. It was all I could do to convene the school community for a discussion of tolerance. I told the story of how prejudice and ethnic hatred had torn my family asunder, how the people I knew and loved were lost in its deadly fire. I made a plea to the students and teachers to avoid the traps that so many before them had fallen into, to embrace each other's differences. The cost of allowing hate to fester was too great.

Then I did what I'd always done—I spent my afternoons on the ground, checking in on students in the bus lines and on the basketball courts, trying to help stamp out conflicts before they bubbled over. At this point, my job wasn't confined to any particular district, so I found myself traveling to South Boston and Charlestown, Mattapan and Roxbury. After falling for years, truancy was becoming higher than ever. With neighborhoods dividing into factions, police divided in their loyalties, and teenagers roamed the streets instead of attending school, I feared the city could explode into riots at any moment.

Kids formed into makeshift gangs and confronted others with curses and epithets. Bats, knives, improvised clubs became unavoidable accessories. The police who patrolled the streets were often viewed as the enemy— by people both white and black. Most politicians begged for peace, but some chose to be divisive and fomented anger. That was like holding a match at the scene of a gas tanker accident. It was a kind of foolishness I'd only seen once before.

I would do my best to push back against the hatred and bigotry block by block.

In South Boston I tried to turn a rock fight into a discussion. Shuttling between the two groups and asking them to stand down, I told them I'd leave them alone if they took a break to meet each other, and when they did, two of the members recognized each other as old playground acquaintances. They might never be friends again, but they seemed to have enough respect for each other to agree to disagree and leave it at that. Though the wariness would continue, I was glad to discover some common ground.

Mattapan was different. The problems in that neighborhood weren't so much about busing dividing the community as they were about the absenteeism spurred by the busing crisis. All the teenagers who had dropped out of school had altered the landscape. Drinking and drugs were everywhere and threatened the fabric of the community. What once had been a thriving enclave had dissolved into poverty and disrepair as the mass exodus to the suburbs had left many storefronts vacant and homes abandoned.

For months Jeremiah E. Burke High School was a frequent stop I'd make. I used basketball and baseball as tools to help bring kids together, and found teachers and administrators to give me support and serve as my eyes when I was elsewhere.

I spent time in the other affected communities as well, and sought to meet new students—as well as checking in with those I knew best to get the pulse of communities—whenever tensions seemed to spike. As it always proves to be when a community makes a shift and is forced to confront its own history of racism, change was slow and painful, but it was inevitable. As the years passed and police presence dwindled, the reality that integrated schools would offer better opportunities for all finally took hold in people's consciousness. Racial tensions and prejudice did not disappear, of course—nor would the absenteeism, or the surprise acts of violence on school grounds that would occasionally strike and send me into a panic—but at least we would be giving our children the equality we promised them.

I also advocated for change on the top level, calling in all the favors I had to stand up to the Boston School Committee, which refused to accept integration.

The glimmers of love and acceptance continued to be all too rare, but the ones I saw inspired me. They were proof that despite humans' unmatched capacity for hatred, bigotry, brutality, and murder, the slide into chaos of my nightmares—a path that begins with individual assaults and ends with genocide—is never inevitable. We are never so far down the path of violence that no community can stand up and stop it.

Chapter 33

Guns in the Distance

Dachau
Date uncertain

How I was saved from being burned with the pile of corpses is a mystery to me. Why whoever approached the mass grave and pulled me to safety did not get shot or hanged, no one ever told me. No record, no testimony can tell me if it was in the night, a clandestine approach, or if there was a diversion planted for the guards that gave a prisoner an opening to reach me. All I know is that I was saved from being cremated alive, and I owe someone—or perhaps many people—my gratitude.

No one spoke of it for fear of enraging a guard or the commandant, but as winter began to wane, the low hum of artillery in the distance filtered into the barracks. Though some initially weren't sure what the soft rumbling was, so long had we been inside the camps, others began to spread word that it was the fight approaching, that the Nazis were down on their backs. With the dark of night came a stillness that allowed us to hear the artillery more clearly.

We knew that the guards heard it, too, and whenever the ground began to shake their faces immediately transformed, fierce expressions becoming overcome with fear. They glanced nervously at each other, as if to ask, What now?

Soon I began to find helmets and tunics lying near the gates, shed by guards as they tried to make an escape. Within weeks, planes could be heard overhead as well, the whistle of bombs falling from the fuselages onto Hitler's army. On more than one morning we woke to see guards who had tried to leave hanging from the same barbed wire that was designed to keep us in, their limp corpses shot in several places.

"They will never let us be found," someone said through tears as the camp lights dimmed one evening to keep the location out of sight of the surveillance of the planes overhead.

I believed it was true. How could they allow the world to see these camps, the mass graves, the records of the children they had killed, the Jews, intellectuals, and artists—some with sizable followings before the Holocaust—who remained here. Being exposed meant they would be jailed, humiliated, and forced to face their consciences.

"They will burn the whole place," someone said in a raspy voice. His pants were dirty, tattered, and far too large. "I saw the shovels leaving the camp this morning. One mass grave for all of us."

We sat and waited, listening for the planes and gunfire. We were weaponless and so weak we didn't know what we could do. Eventually, we decided collectively that we would pray that our deaths would not be in vain—that when someone arrived to end this madness, there would be some evidence that we had been there and of what they'd done to us. Cleaning up this mess completely would be impossible. Our lost brothers and sisters—perhaps even all of us, too—would be a warning to others of what could occur, what mankind was capable of doing when hateful violence went without an answer.

Weeping filled the barrack. Over the coming days, I also remember love overflowing.

"Thank you for trying so hard," I'd hear someone whisper.

"I love you."

"We will be remembered."

Chapter 34

To Never Forget

Walking toward the doors of the Boston City Hall, it struck me for the first time what an odd structure it was. Set on a large promenade just off the central business district, it rises above the pavement as if it had been built in disparate sections, then pieced together haphazardly by a hurried architect. Around it stands buildings dating to colonial times that are destinations for tourists from around the world. Faneuil Hall, where American revolutionaries such as Samuel Adams and James Otis rallied their comrades to fight their British oppressors, is there, just across Congress Street, and people gather at the site to eat and be entertained by street performers. The Bunker Hill Monument, attesting to one of the first victories of the War of Independence, rises in the distance, and the Old North Church, where lanterns were hung to warn of the approaching British soldiers, is a short walk away.

I walked into the nearly colorless modernist edifice at the center of all of these treasures that pumps the lifeblood of the city. I had been summoned here by the mayor, Ray Flynn, who had sent me a cryptic note asking to talk. I'd risen high in the city's community centers, and as I approached my sixtieth birthday I wondered if perhaps Flynn wanted me to retire and give someone new a shot. The truth was that even though I never stopped being inspired by my students, I had begun to look forward to the day when I'd have more time to spend with my family.

I worried, too, that my ventures into high school auditoriums had reached the end of their shelf life. I had told my story so many times and in so many different forums that I started to wonder if I would know when my speeches had become stale, and whether students only listened to me in order to be polite. It had been nearly fifty years since I'd left Dachau—was that long enough to forget, to neatly package the trauma I'd endured and store it deep inside me as I had initially tried to when I came to America?

As shocking as the Boston City Hall's exterior architecture is, the inside was even more confusing, with stairways and elevator shafts leading you into corners and utility rooms, half floors spilling onto unused space near the front entrance. Precious little light was able to penetrate the fortress-like windows to help you find your way, and the intermittent fluorescent fixtures, many of them filled with dead bulbs, were of little help. When I'd first come here, many years earlier, Kevin White was mayor.

I had to ask at the information desk how to get to the mayor's office. "Third floor through the back elevator over there, down the hall to the right, and in the back."

There were several desks lining the path leading there, and at the last one sat a police officer, who nodded and smiled, waving me ahead into a waiting room. I sat there, resting my elbows on the overstuffed armchairs, and while I waited, I mused.

My children were grown now. Mike was interested in politics and had mentioned running for a council seat at some point. Julie had enrolled in law school. They'd both heard my stories over and over, and I worried that like their mother they would tire of me and find solace elsewhere. My past had made me a frustratingly insistent person at times—I was sure it had cost me my marriage—but my relentlessness was important because it also came from my certainty about what was right. I was devoted utterly to the causes that I believed in, steadfast in delivering my messages: This can never happen again; get an education; recognize the opportunities afforded to you as an American citizen, no matter how much of an outsider you feel, and pursue them like they're the lifeline that they are. "The mayor will see you now, Mr. Ross." A woman was standing over me, motioning for me to follow.

The mayor's office was full of dark wood and plush carpets. There was a stillness inside that surprised me, a quiet that seemed to shut out the world beyond his door. His desk was large and had several documents spread about it so evenly that they looked like props. I wondered if one of them had to do with me.

Mayor Flynn was on the phone when I entered and motioned for me to sit. Then he looked out the window as he finished his conversation. He was a sturdy man with broad shoulders and a thick neck. His hair was brown but had started to gray, and his shirt clung to his arms and chest.

He soon put down the phone.

"Mr. Ross," he said, extending a hand, "I'm Ray Flynn."

"It is an honor to see you again, sir," I said. "We've met several times at events about the children, and once at a ceremony about... well, about the Holocaust. Perhaps you remember."

"I do, of course," he said. "Well, thank you for coming. I have been meaning to have you up here to chat. Do you know why you're here?"

"No, sir, but whatever you need I am willing to help."

A wide smile filtered over his expression, and he nodded in acknowledgment. He seemed to be contemplating what to say next.

"Am I no longer useful?" I asked. "Maybe I talk too much about the past?"

"Oh my, no," he said. "No, not at all."

He came and sat beside me. "I wanted to have you here to thank you. I've been in office for years, and nearly every day someone comes in and has an anecdote about you—you helping get their kids to love one of their teachers or helping someone who made a mistake and found himself in jail. You're a legend in this building!"

I couldn't help but laugh nervously.

"I've waited too long," he said. "I should have had you here a long time ago. You've been doing this a long time, I understand."

"Thank you, Mr. Mayor." I told him that I'd always loved my work.

"Please," he said. "Ray."

I nodded.

The room darkened slightly, as if the sun had ducked behind a cloud.

"Listen," he said. "The city owes you a debt of gratitude. We want to do something for you so that you know how much you're appreciated. Maybe a ceremony for you with all the kids you've helped or a plaque we could put here in city hall. I don't want to embarrass you, and frankly

I can tell right now that you're easily embarrassed, but I must do something on behalf of the city, and I won't take no for an answer."

My mind rushed. I leaned back in my chair, looking up to the ceiling and taking a deep breath to compose myself. I had a thought I'd long treasured but shared with no one, knowing I'd be unable to deal with the disappointment of having it beaten down. Now I could feel it finding its voice.

"To tell you the truth, Ray, there is something I'd like." I cleared my throat and took another breath. "Forgive me for taking my time with this. It's something very important to me."

"Name it," he said.

I nodded. "I'd like to create a Holocaust memorial here in Boston. Something special, something memorable, something that will be here forever so that we never forget what happened. Other cities have done it, and I don't want Boston to be left behind. We have a lot of survivors here who can be an enormous support. I can canvass and find us financing."

The mayor sat back in his chair.

"Why, of course," he said, as if he was appalled there wasn't a memorial in the city already. "Of course. Of course."

We sat without speaking for a moment, contemplating what we were about to embark upon.

"Do you know where you'd like it to be?" he asked. "Have you thought about that?"

It turned out I had—I'd had more than four decades grappling with my experience in the streets of Boston to consider it. I stood and walked to the window looking down on Congress Street toward Faneuil Hall.

"There," I said.

He stood beside me. "Where?"

"There," I repeated, pointing now to the small rectangular park just below. "Right there in the middle of everything, where people will see it when they go out for their lunch breaks and tourists will pass as they walk to Faneuil Hall."

The mayor studied the prominent location. His silence made me sure I'd overstepped.

"Perhaps it's too much to ask," I said. "I know how difficult it is to get projects approved here, how many people want to have a say."

He was silent.

He smiled an unreadable, flat smile.

"That," he said, "is perfect. It's done. This office will not rest until we make this happen."

Chapter 35

Memorial Rising

Boston
October 22, 1995

Other than my children and the work to which I devoted my career in the city schools, the New England Holocaust Memorial is the single achievement of which I am most proud. My work with kids of all ages, races, and nationalities in the city, my efforts to lift people out of poverty, and my devotion to troubled neighborhoods all make me feel a surge of gratification. Still, it is the memorial that I know will live on past my years and speak to people for generations to come. The message there is clear: Here is what happened to us. Here is what we can never allow to happen again.

At the memorial, six towers rise high over the landscape, and the glass panels that make up the structures' walls are each etched with tens of thousands of numbers just like the one still tattooed on my arm. Each tower is dedicated to one of the death camps, and a quote from someone imprisoned there is carved into the stone tiles along it. Steam rises like a horrifying deadly gas from dark vents beneath each tower.

The dedication ceremony felt as if it was joyful, and at the same time sad for anyone who lost loved ones in the Holocaust. For me, it also felt like a final testament to my work in the city. Images from the years I'd spent in the school system flashed in my head, every speech, every time I donned my prison clothing, every time I convinced a child to go to school instead of wandering the streets.

Elie Wiesel was there, and I'd like to think every survivor in Boston came as well. Mayor Menino gave a speech, and the architect—the magnificent Stanley Saitowitz— was lauded. Mike and Julie were there holding my hands while I waited for my chance to take the podium as the final dedication speaker.

When I did, I knew exactly what to say.

"My name was Szmulek Rozental," I began, "and I was born at the wrong time, in the wrong place, in the wrong country. I was a man before I was a boy. But I am here today. I have been beaten over and over again until I was believed to be dead, but I am here. The Nazis starved me until they nearly did kill me. They beat me up and shattered my teeth because I was hungry enough to take a potato from their barrack. One guard raped me until I longed for death. But they couldn't stamp out my spirit. They would never stamp out any of our spirits—even those of the millions of people whom they killed. They tried their best to kill us and to kill our religion, and many of our brethren died, and while we remember them—while we *must* remember them—every day, here we are. Our religion is still alive, and their religion of fear and hate is not.

"My name is now Steve Ross, but Szmulek Rozental, the boy born sixty-four years ago in Lodz, Poland, is still very much with me. I am a survivor."

Chapter 36

Liberation

Dachau
April 29, 1945

The US Army soldiers flooded our camp in a rush. The German guards who remained had put down their guns, and with the tide turned, these defeated men squatted in subservient repose as our liberators opened the doors to the barracks and let the prisoners file into the yards.

No matter what these Allied soldiers had seen to that point, what they found at Dachau was more than many could take. As they watched us limp into the open—broken, beaten, emaciated, and filthy—many of them broke down, many of them were sickened, and the weeping and breathless gasps were pervasive. Perhaps it is human nature that some simply turned on the Germans and assassinated them with quick shots to the head. Others, realizing a reckoning would come later, tried to hold back the rage that was building with each passing minute.

It was not long before others came into the camp. Doctors and nurses, truckers with food and water, more military personnel, journalists and cameramen. They all struggled to make sense of what was before them. The medical people tried to comfort me, but I was so sick and so brutalized, and there were so many others like me to tend to, that I think when they realized I would survive they finally gave up trying to provide any consolation. The triage continued with scores of relief workers going from person to person to see who might be saved and who was beyond hope, most softly crying as they moved down the lines.

Other than the few hours I spent sleeping in a pile of dead bodies, this was the one time in my life I felt I had given up. What should have been a reason for rejoicing was instead a clarion call to just end my suffering. I could go now easily, quietly, without having to endure any more pain, any more hunger. No one would care or probably even notice—after all, it was possible that everyone I had ever loved was dead. I would later learn that with the single exception of Herzil, that was the case.

If I simply let go now and allowed my heart to stop beating, someone, I thought, would at least bury me and perhaps make a note somewhere, cataloging me in the annals of the horrors that had occurred. Perhaps someone would give them my name or perhaps they'd list me by the number tattooed on my arm.

My spirit was so exhausted that I decided the only thing for me to do was to walk myself to death.

And so, with the gates now open and the chaos of the most horrifying rescue imaginable unfolding in the only way it could, I simply wandered away. Turning out of the gate in a choice made wholly at random, I limped along the open road that wended off in the distance to a destination unknown and a fate I cared little about. My legs and mouth still ached from the beating I'd endured. My feet were crooked, the skin cracked. I could see the way before me, but the poundings I'd taken had left me with floating black marks crossing my vision, and blinking still hurt from the swelling.

Others had also left the camp—perhaps after being imprisoned so long it was a compulsion we couldn't suppress—and they struggled as I did as we moved down the roadway. Most were single travelers like me, hunched and staggering, and wandering aimlessly, but a few had found companions to walk with, each leaning on the other for stability and strength. It was a parade of attrition, all of us walking toward death pushed by the relief that we knew would come with the final moments of surrender. And indeed, as I moved farther and farther from camp, my perceptions were confirmed. Dead bodies of prisoners who'd dropped as they walked came more and more frequently into view along the road, the corpses lying just off the pavement, the knees of some drawn to their chests as if they sought a final embrace and could only hug themselves.

Dead soldiers, too, became increasingly prevalent. Some appeared to have been killed recently, blood still fresh from mortal wounds, but others seemed to have already rotted, their skin decomposing, their eyes black, their uniforms picked clean of anything that might be useful. I stared at all of them as I passed and wondered whether there would be an effort sometime to bury these dead and whether, in the end, they would be interred with the prisoners. Bile rose in my throat for an instant, but the emotion disappeared as fast as it had come. What difference did it make at this point? The wheels of justice were in motion, and my mission was to put one foot in front of the other until I no longer could.

That night I spent shivering in the burned remains of a house just off the road. Where I lay, the roof had collapsed into a pile of charred boards and rafters, but the pocket between the standing brick and debris kept the wind at bay and allowed me a few moments of rest. In between the intermittent periods of sleep, I thought about my brothers and sisters and my parents, and I thought about whether I'd ever see any of them again, or if not about how much pain they'd endured before they died. I also thought about Pinia and how he thought I was special somehow, how, in his eyes, I would no doubt survive and tell everyone what happened. I knew then that if I was ever going to survive this, I would devote my life to helping children. I could never go back and help Pinia make it through. To help boys and girls like him was the next best thing.

By midday I was certain the end was near. I hadn't eaten in so long I could hardly recall any food ever passing my lips, the only image I could muster being the potato for which I'd been beaten, rolling slowly away from my outstretched hand. My legs had grown even more wobbly, and I peered ahead along the road for the place to finally stop, to lay myself in a grass-covered pitch and close my eyes for the last time.

But there was something else on the road in the distance: a column of men and vehicles, black smoke spewing above them. I started to hear the steady rumbling of their engines. I stopped and studied the convoy as it moved toward me, and I could see that it was massive. Hundreds of men and countless vehicles moved seemingly in unison. I knew by their colors that they were not Germans, but I had no idea who they were.

The first soldiers reached me and passed, and while a few looked over and stared they didn't stop. Hundreds more passed and still the line seemed to go off into the distance beyond the reach of my vision. For what seemed like hours the procession continued, and I stood quietly wondering where they were going and what awaited them when they got there.

Startling me, shouts rang out and ran up and down the lines. With a slowing of momentum, then, the men stopped, the vehicles ground to a halt, and the engines ebbed and finally went silent. Two tanks in front of me skidded on their tracks and emitted a final blast of exhaust, and around them the men ambled in small circles appearing, at first, not sure what to do. Then, removing their helmets, they sat in groups of three or four, their backs against the underpinnings of the tanks. Few of them spoke. Some let their heads fall back as they closed their eyes.

I didn't move, not because I didn't want to but more because I felt paralyzed. If these men killed me, ran me over, shot me, so be it. If after a while they moved on, all the better. This was as good a spot as any for the nightmare to end, as good a final memory as I could expect.

A rusty metal screech drew my attention to the top of the tank in front of me. I squinted to see the hatch opening and a hand, followed by an arm and a shoulder, reaching toward the sky. A man pulled himself up, shrugged, and sat with his legs dangling still in the tank. He stretched and shook as if to wipe away a fog. I watched him peer around, straining his neck to see the column behind him before taking in several long breaths.

He then pulled up a pack from below and rested it at his hip. Reaching inside the pack, he searched for a moment before extracting a can.

Loud voices below startled me. I ignored them, still watching the man atop the tank, who was eating now, using his knife and its flat silvery blade to spoon whatever was in the can into his mouth. I stared. He chewed, and took a long swig from his canteen.

That's when he saw me. He wiped his mouth with his sleeve as he set the water down. His eyes narrowed. He looked as if he was disoriented and chastened at once; surprised and appalled that I was sitting alone and that no one had even noticed I was there.

I didn't move as we continued to try to make sense of each other.

Swinging his legs up from the hatch, he jumped from the turret to the base and then to the ground, dust rising from his boots when he landed. I noticed then that he looked at once robust and also tired. His face was shaven, his uniform wrinkled, the sleeves torn partially at the shoulders. He had eyes that reminded me of my father, glassy and broad, and his chin was pockmarked like a golf ball. He walked toward me.

Despite my years of conditioning at the hands of the Nazi guards, I knew by now that this man would not harm me. He walked gingerly, gently, quietly, as if to ask permission to come near. I didn't move.

Standing over me, he said something in a near whisper in a language I did not understand. Then he sat on the ground beside me. Somehow I knew what he was trying to say. Somehow his presence, the warmth that emanated from him, the aura he gave off, made me breathe more deeply, more evenly than since I'd left the camp.

He lifted his hand toward me and presented the can, still filled with food. What it was, I didn't know, but it smelled musky and salty and had a lovely reddish color that I couldn't recall seeing in years. I took the can in my hand.

He watched me as I spooned the substance into my mouth in eager fingerfuls. Quiet at first, after a few moments he began to speak and though, again, I had no idea what the dialogue meant, I instinctively knew he was telling me to slow down, to calm myself, that everything was going to be better now, that I was going to be all right.

He produced another can from his pocket and with a quick movement of his knife opened it. That, too, was placed in my hand and that, too, was consumed in gulps, leaving only my fingers and thumb, which I proceeded to lick clean.

Across the road, some of his friends chided him, obviously laughing at him for his generosity, waving their hands at him to give up on this lost cause. He bellowed back and they demurred but shrugged almost in unison. He stared at me then with dread, and though no words were spoken I knew he was wondering what had happened to me. Maybe word had come down through the ranks of what lay ahead in Dachau. This was the moment it all came into focus for him.

Orders were shouted up and down the lines, but before he lifted himself he took my arm and squeezed it in a way that I knew was asking me to try to be strong, to survive. His eyes were piercing as he stared and something inside me—my capitulation—dissolved and was replaced with a strength that I'd not felt in more months than I could recall. He glanced back at me a couple of times as he rose and sauntered back to his tank. As he was about to climb aboard, he staggered, as if changing his mind. Standing over me again, a moment later, he reached deep into his jacket and fumbled inside.

"American," he said, pulling out a cloth folded neatly in his hand. He handed it to me. "American," he repeated.

Unfolding what he'd given me, I studied it. Blue in one corner with stars and perfect red and white stripes down the side and at the bottom, I found it beautiful, striking really. As I rubbed it with my fingers, something inside me stirred. My resolve tightened and a nearly overwhelming energy like a life force of hope surged inside me. I turned back up to him, but he was already climbing back up to his turret, barking at the others to move along.

I waved my flag until they disappeared into the distance.

Acknowledgments

I arrived in this country with nothing and with no one. My brother Herzil came a few years later. Everything I achieved—my freedom, my education, my career, my family, the memorial, this book—all of it came from this great country. Some are losing faith in this country, and when I see acts like the vandalism of the memorial in the summer of 2017, I can understand why. But I hope this book illustrates, among many other things, why I will never lose my faith in it.

This book began with countless sessions, over many months, with my dear friend John Horgan, a Boston-based teacher and historian, who sat with me and tirelessly chronicled my story. That research served as a vital tool in the writing of this book when my own memory needed support.

Acknowledgments

Thankfully, that research landed in the hands of Glenn Frank, a Boston-based attorney and author who agreed to take this project on. He perfectly captured my voice in a way that no one else could. His attention to every detail and the time he poured into this project to bring my story to life make me proud to have had the fortune to collaborate with him.

I want to thank former US Ambassador to the Vatican Raymond Flynn, who wrote the foreword to this book, for his support over these years. Together we worked in Boston's Youth Activities Commission administering to at-risk youth. I believe everyone who lives in the city, and even those who visit, is in his debt for giving us the land to build the New England Holocaust Memorial in the heart of Boston.

Brian Wallace wasn't just one of those kids that I was able to help many years ago; like so many of them who were counted out, he defied the naysayers and launched an extraordinary career as a public servant, becoming the Massachusetts state representative for his native South Boston. It was Brian, with the help of John and Denise Dow and our wonderful agent Ike Williams, who got this story into the hands of our publisher and who helped confirm countless details in many of the Boston anecdotes told in the book.

And throughout my life, and especially during this process, there has been Alan Eisner, the former editor-in-chief of the *Boston Herald.* I knew Alan as a young man growing up in Boston. He's one of many who became part of my broader family and eventually more like a son. His efforts put together the team that made this book a reality. Without him, it would not have happened.

I thoroughly enjoyed working with the team at Hachette Books, including our editor David Lamb, publicist Joanna Pinsker, and marketer Odette Fleming, who each handled this project with the care it deserved.

Throughout my adult life I've had a family that has supported me unconditionally. Sadly, my life's partner, Mary, wasn't able to see this book published. But it was her love and support that allowed me to realize giant dreams like the Holocaust memorial, and she was next to me when my grandson Joseph, named after my father, was born. I think of her all the time.

My two children, Julie and Michael, are my greatest joy. They have supported me endlessly and have made me proud.

As I've grown older, I've needed more and more help getting around. There is a team of friends and caregivers who keep me going. I'm grateful for the kindness that they have shown me.

Others have contributed in different ways. Roger Lyons's tireless work resulted in an award-winning documentary about my life. His film served as an opportunity to gather lifelong friends and family, including fellow

SEP 0 5 2018

DAUPHIN COUNTY LIBRARY SYSTEM